I0487385

Practical Public Relations for the Small Business: Tools and Tactics for Competitive Advantage

Dave Skocik
MA, APR

iUniverse, Inc.
New York   Bloomington

Practical Public Relations for the Small Business: Tools and Tactics for Competitive Advantage

Copyright © 2008, 2009 by David V. Skocik.

All rights reserved. No part of this book may be used or reproduced by any means, graphic, electronic, or mechanical, including photocopying, recording, taping or by any information storage retrieval system without the written permission of the publisher except in the case of brief quotations embodied in critical articles and reviews.

The views expressed in this work are solely those of the author and do not necessarily reflect the views of the publisher, and the publisher hereby disclaims any responsibility for them.

iUniverse books may be ordered through booksellers or by contacting:

iUniverse
1663 Liberty Drive
Bloomington, IN 47403
www.iuniverse.com
1-800-Authors (1-800-288-4677)

Because of the dynamic nature of the Internet, any Web addresses or links contained in this book may have changed since publication and may no longer be valid. The views expressed in this work are solely those of the author and do not necessarily reflect the views of the publisher, and the publisher hereby disclaims any responsibility for them.

ISBN: 978-0-595-44623-0 (pbk)
ISBN: 978-0-595-88947-1 (ebk)

Printed in the United States of America

iUniverse rev. date: 2/17/2009

Some Comments

"*Practical PR is a great read. It provides quick, entertaining facts and examples. It is not only full of information, but also full of recommended actions you can implement today. Practical PR is both useful and "practical" for all those in the business world. It is an excellent business resource.*"

Judy Diogo, President, Central Delaware Chamber of Commerce

"*This book will help anyone achieve a competitive edge in today's market. It is a great source of sound advice on how to implement effective communication, whether they are just starting out or wish to reinvent their approach to the public.*"

Mimi LeComte, Chiropractor

"*If you are determined to make your small business dreams a reality, you will be well served by this book. Practical Public Relations is a great resource of real-life, results oriented insights: time-tested and proven. You can ill afford to forgo applying these principles to your business – do it today!*"

Greg Makosky, Owner, Money Mailer of Central Delaware

"*Sincere appreciation to you for your good work in compiling a lifetime of essential knowledge. Your insight and perspective serves to provide a master class and primer for newly minted entrepreneurs as well as seasoned business people. The easy to read style and format are most welcome.*"

Gregory F. Mazzotta, Malcolm Baldrige Quality Award examiner

"*Having been in small business four times in my career I can attest that this book carefully emphasizes the critical needs and actions needed by an entrepreneur to succeed. I have used many of these practices myself with great success. My compliments to Dave Skocik for this thoughtful endeavor.*"

Fred Rohm, past executive director, New Castle County, (Delaware) Chamber of Commerce

Practical Public Relations
for the Small Business:
Tools and Tactics for Competitive Advantage

"It is not enough that a man has clearness of vision, and reliance on sincerity, he must also have the art of expression, or he will remain obscure."

George H. Lewes, author, philosopher

Contents

Forward

This primer is an attempt to explain the rules of the road for entrepreneurs who would like earned (free) publicity for themselves and their businesses.

It is a project that resulted from scribbled notes over many years working with people. That's not because of its complexity or length. Rather, it is the result of a long series of stops, starts, and rewrites as I put it aside for other priorities.

Of course, being in the information age makes one realize there can never be a completion of anything having to do with the distribution of information, only updates on new ideas for getting the word out. Therefore, to wait is to fall further behind.

However, while technology changes on a daily basis, basic human relations skills like courtesy and consideration for others never go out of style.

As a professional public relations practitioner, I have been regularly asked for advice and help on projects. The simple fact is that many who run small businesses can't afford to employ a public relations pro and have to guess at what works.

This work is the result of many conversations with fellow business people in my travels and with non-profit organizations in my adopted home town of Dover, Delaware.

As it progressed it became clear it is largely a recitation of best practices from many entrepreneurs and friends I've worked with and have come to know over the years. As such, this is not a textbook with academic citations but rather a narrative of informational comments derived from lessons learned.

The people on the cover represent a small portion of the talented and creative entrepreneurs I've come to know. This work is designed to provide an insight into how reporters and editors of print and electronic media judge what is worthy of coverage.

Dave Skocik, MA, APR

Dover, Delaware 2009

"Human relations are built on feeling, not on reason or knowledge. And feeling is not an exact science; like all spiritual qualities, it has the vagueness of greatness about it."

Amelia E. Barr, teacher, author

Good public relations, like human relations, is a process, not an event.

This has been my credo for more than 25 years in public relations. It is also the theme of this work.

The intent of this short primer is to provide basic information about communicating with your current and prospective customers or clients. It is an eclectic compilation of tips, ideas and processes based on experience rather than an attempt to provide in-depth counsel on any specific issue or problem.

For ease of reading I've created six general categories of information in this book, which is a compilation of education (from my instructors as well as later from my students and clients), learned conventions, experience and, I hope, wisdom acquired through working with so many smart and interesting people over the years.

I've told my PR students the only equation they would have to know for my class is Visibility = Credibility. But human relations is a broader concept than public relations, because it relies on the same principle of treating people honestly and fairly.

It is summed up in Rotary International's simple Four-Way Test, created in 1932 by Rotarian Herbert J. Taylor when asked to take charge of a company facing bankruptcy.

The 24-word, four question test for employees to follow in their business and professional lives became the guide for sales, production, advertising, and all relations with dealers and customers. The survival of the company is credited to this simple philosophy.

It has been translated into more than a hundred languages. It asks the following four questions:

"Of the things we think, say or do:

1. Is it the truth?

2. Is it fair to all concerned?

3. Will it build goodwill and better friendships?

4. Will it be beneficial to all concerned?"

Can you imagine how much better the world would be if we all operated by these principles?

On Public Relations

"The public is the only critic whose opinion is worth anything at all."
Mark Twain, aka Samuel Clemens, literary icon

Public relations is as much of an art as a science because it deals in perception and ongoing interaction with internal and external audiences. I've sprinkled quotes throughout the text to illustrate how people from every walk of life are concerned about communicating effectively with others, for we are all judged not only by what we say, but by how we say it.

Edward L. Bernays, considered the father of public relations, in 1923 wrote "Crystallizing Public Opinion," in which he described public relations as an applied social science. He believed public relations should be professionalized and licensed.

Bernays' uncle and role model was Sigmund Freud, the father of psychoanalysis. He used Freud's insights into the psyche to design his PR campaigns. While his famous uncle believed in getting people to talk about their psychoses, Bernays believed in working behind the scenes to subtly shift public opinion in favor of a client's cause.

In his third book in 1928, he claimed, "The new profession of public relations has grown up because of the increasing complexity of modern life and the consequent necessity of making the actions of one part of the public understandable to other sectors of the public." The title of that book was "This Business of Propaganda," which not only played a key role in America's wartime strategy, but also found a proponent in Hitler's propaganda minister Joseph Goebbels.

I've owned several small businesses and worked with businesspeople for many years and know that PR is not only about your business, but also yourself. This guide incorporates the challenges and the how-to of basic business public relations and touches on the philosophy of human interaction from a personal perspective.

Dave Skocik

1

In General

The Basics

It's the information age! There is no better time to communicate with others.

We have never had more information channeled to us. But while we have more access to information, no one has added any more time to our day.

That means the majority of messages are ignored as we reach information overload. Some estimate we receive as many as 2,000 messages per day.

Traditional messengers include TV commercials; news programs with crawling messages; celebrities who endorse products; billboards; radio; voice-mail; surveys; phone solicitations; signs on trucks, buses and cabs; magazines; posters; billing statements; newspapers; grocery carts; airport walkways; flyers; coupons; pop ups; computer screen links; handouts; telephone hold messages; cell phone ads; and even the proverbial matchbook cover introducing us to art school – the original way of "getting the picture."

This is particularly true of candidates for political office. Once they've identified voters (or customers), successful communicators probe for underlying issues to address rather than repeat the same memorized talking points. They also seek out the undecided voters they need to win rather than continue talking to supporters.

Connecting the right issue to the right audience establishes the personal relationships necessary to build understanding and trust. Additionally, candidates should make certain their campaign images and messages - verbal, printed and electronic – all align.

Business owners can learn from the furious and focused activities of political camps. They include websites, emails, blogs, radio, TV and print ads, phone surveys, events, personal visits, postcards, push cards, lawn signs, brochures, polls, letters, position papers, rallies, interviews, personal appearances, debates, fund raisers, and affiliations with other groups.

While campaign activities are relatively short-lived and don't apply per se to business, their tactics are instructive because businesses must target their own customers and prospects. Like politicians, it's a struggle not only to win new people to their side, but to keep the old ones. Both in politics and business, affinity groups are golden.

It should also be noted that promoting a candidate is more akin to marketing (selling a product) than is public relations, which is a long-term institutional approach more aligned with the needs of businesses.

Of course, people actively seek information. As of this writing in early 2009, there are 31 billion searches on Google each month. The lesson here is that communicators must be more precise and better than ever to get their messages across.

What's the difference between public relations and marketing?

Public relations is a process that focuses on long term results rather than short term gains.

It is a planned series of activities and events to positively portray a person, business, idea, institution or other entity to its publics.

In the example of a business, its publics include external groups directly affected by the business and its activities as well as those who can exert influence on the business. Internal audiences, like employees and family members, are also important to consider.

Unlike marketing, which is often short-term and concerns a specific product rollout, public relations is most successful when planned and funded as an ongoing part of the business plan and institutional vision.

If it is to maintain credibility public relations should never to be used to manipulate or deceive its public(s). PR should be, in a very real sense, the conscience of the organization. The PR professional must sometimes play the "devil's advocate" and question business decisions he or she believes will have negative consequences, not only on the bottom line, but on the organization's reputation.

Sometimes even well-intentioned actions go astray. Unintended consequences of a decision are called backlash. More about that later.

If the organization is to outlive its founders then ethics and morality must always be a consideration in dealing with the public. That applies whether one is a full time professional or someone creating a public perception of his or her own small business.

H. Irving Grousbeck, a managing partner of the Boston Celtics and co-director of the Center for Entrepreneurial Studies at Stanford Business School, teaches that individuals should pursue entrepreneurship by taking the "high road," acting in an ethical fashion and taking a long-term view by asking how they want to be remembered at the end of their lives.

In a very real sense public relations is about keeping the process honest. It is a process driven by need, powered by specific intent and guided by received wisdom and new information.

Marketing, unlike the broad, institutional view of public relations, has a product specific focus. It includes research to determine the need for new or repackaged existing products, who the target audiences will be, the best features and benefits to promote, and what messages will be most effective. Incorporated into this planning is an analysis of the competition. That's why some marketing strategies directly compare products.

When the product is released, marketing then implements its plan to promote it, most often through paid advertising.

Publicity is also generated through press releases, interviews, public events and press conferences. For publicity to be effective, the media must cooperate by carrying the information provided. Having a positive relationship with local reporters or editors is invaluable.

Put another way, marketing is about achieving competitive advantage in the marketplace.

Some thoughts on a personal, local and national level

"All the president is, is a glorified public relations man who spends his time flattering, kissing, and kicking people to get them to do what they are supposed to do anyway."

Harry S. Truman, US President

"If one morning I walked on top of the water across the Potomac River, the headline that afternoon would read PRESIDENT CAN'T SWIM."

Lyndon B. Johnson, US President

The foregoing quotes emphasize that even presidents, who have enormous influence and legions of professional communicators on their payroll, can become as frustrated as anyone else in effectively getting their messages across.

Public relations goes beyond promoting one's business. <u>At its core is personal relations.</u> In *Ziglar on Selling*, motivational speaker and marketing guru Zig Ziglar says you can never be too prepared for a sales presentation. "The first few seconds you're on the phone will set the stage, mood and atmosphere of the presentation, so have a plan."

How precisely you sell yourself to others may determine whether you and your pitch will be heard. But whether you are what you purport to be will determine your success.

Successful businesses are nearly always run by people who care about others, operate ethically, and are generous. They are likeable and of good humor. Even more to the point, most small business entrepreneurs operate in a small city or town setting and are very often equated personally with their businesses.

Peter Drucker, writer, management consultant and university professor, put it succinctly: "Quality in a product or service is not what the supplier puts in. It is what the customer gets out and is willing to pay for. A product is not quality because it is hard to make and costs a lot of money, as manufacturers typically believe. This is incompetence. Customers pay only for what is of use to them and gives them value. Nothing else constitutes quality."

In other words, we often choose to buy products and services based on <u>who's selling them.</u> That's why some mom & pop stores successfully compete against megastores offering lower prices and bigger inventories.

4

On a local level some advertisers, like auto dealers, are intentionally loud. Their message is to "come on down. **Now!**" There is no more clear call to action than car ads. While screaming announcers irritate us, they know they will grab the attention of people shopping for cars, particularly when discounts are being offered.

Others, like Geico Insurance, take a more innovative approach, alternating ads with their spokes lizard, a caveman, celebrities and offbeat angles and messages that seem to change weekly. Unless you have millions to invest, don't do this because it will be too confusing for a short term ad campaign.

Ad reps will offer endless ideas but assess and test them before you commit. By testing I mean running them by your employees, select customers, and probably your spouse. Spouses tend to see through hype and will be honest. Running your ideas past others for feedback is in a sense a poor man's version of a focus group, and will provide insight you hadn't considered. Understand, however, that based on your influence over employees, friends, and family, you may not get the most honest responses.

Advertising is, after all, about your customers. It's why an honest ad rep will sometimes discourage a businessperson who just doesn't project the right image from stepping in front of the camera or acting as the company spokesperson.

The bottom line is to make people understand what you're offering and to trust you as an honest broker.

Timing is everything

"The greatest problem in communication is the illusion that it has been accomplished."

George Bernard Shaw, Irish Playwright

Try to read several newspapers a day, even if it's an online version. Watch local and national news. There may be something happening that relates in some way to your business or service. Think locally and regionally. Keeping your oar in the water with local media can lead to bigger opportunities. This is one of the benefits of staying involved in community organizations.

Think seasonally if your business is affected by the weather. In **Spring** a plant nursery could address proper fertilizer use, planting, pruning or mulching. **Summer** information could deal with tips to reduce the cost of air conditioning or even the importance of checking on elderly neighbors during hot spells. **Fall**'s subject might concern the importance of cleaning rain gutters, fireplaces, or of winterizing autos. **Winter** produces a plethora of opportunities for educating people.

Mediums include websites, radio shows, letters to the editor, or even paid ads. People like businesses that care about them. Hint: When writing a letter to the editor, mention your business but don't oversell yourself. Editors don't like ads disguised as opinion.

Experts willing to make themselves available to the media may find themselves in larger circles or even the national spotlight, if only for a few seconds. Then again, isn't that what Super Bowl advertisers pay millions for?

Thinking creatively

What sets you apart from your competition? What do you offer the customer similar businesses don't? Are your products better? Are your services superior? Is your guarantee more comprehensive? Do you pay more attention to your customers? Can they rely on you in a pinch? These are attributes of successful people.

The Flat Daddy program of the Georgia National Guard is an excellent example of thinking outside the box. This campaign brought positive publicity to the Guard's efforts to help families cope with the absence of deployed parents. The Navy has developed a similar program for Sailors at sea.

Georgia National Guard units created 200 life-size, waist-up posters of deployed members. The photos were pasted on foam board and presented to families. They could be set in a chair at dinner, a child's room at night, and even carried on family outings. Family members, including spouses, reported that though the idea sounded silly at first, the photos provided comfort to the entire family. One wife reported having her "husband" ride to work with her every day.

Maj. Gen. Frank Vavala, adjutant general of the Delaware National Guard, created two foundations to assist the families of Guard members and Reservists who encounter financial difficulties. The foundations receive money from the state and private donors for emergencies.

They have provided cash for basic necessities, utilities, car payments, rent, and unexpected expenses. Made up of a mixture of military and civilian board members, the foundations have made a difference in the lives of those who serve, even forestalling evictions in some cases.

These actions communicate compassion and understanding for others. That's always a good thing. It's what builds good will, reputation, and loyalty.

Although most businesses don't delve as deeply into programs like this, there is always room for identified community service. It might be sponsoring a children's athletic team, a church group, a toys for tots program, or involvement in a public project.

On another level, keep a record of all your customers and let them know when you're having a special sale, even if it's through e-mail. My brother, a top salesman in a men's clothing store, keeps an index file of customers looking for specific items and follows up with a call when what they want becomes available. Most of his customers reciprocate by waiting until he's on duty to buy, even if it means making another trip to the store. Individual attention and loyalty matter.

It also takes a lot less effort and resources to retain your current customers than to find new ones.

- Give your customers an occasional free gift with purchase of your product or service. Every 10th haircut is free at the local Great Clips.

- Sponsor a local kids' athletic team or a patriotic event, or sponsor a fundraiser for a non-profit community service organization.

- Be available to speak at local clubs or community groups. You might even be invited to join.

- Conduct a free public service seminar or partner with someone to do so. Make sure you have information available for attendees and the press.

- Promote events related to the service you offer. Generate a list of people who show interest and ask if you can include them on your regular e-mail list.

- Let local public service organizations, e.g., teachers, military, police or fire stations, know you're offering a discount to their members during a specified period of time. This could be rotated among various groups so there's always a limited sale in progress for specific groups. Specially targeted sales will bring people into your business who may not otherwise stop by.

- If you believe a local organization is doing something worthwhile for the community, write a letter to the editor praising them. It will win friends.

- Sponsor a special event related to your business, perhaps in conjunction with another business or a non-profit organization.

It's a smart man ...

Shakespeare observed that brevity is the soul of wit. A more modern movie version was spoken by Clint Eastwood portraying detective Harry Callahan, aka, "Dirty Harry," when he noted, "it's a smart man who knows his limitations."

Whether you're making statements in a press release or in person, stay within your area of expertise. Though virtually all interview requests concern positive subjects, you may encounter the occasional reporter who brings an agenda. Commenting on contentious subjects or people runs a high risk of getting you in trouble, particularly if you show emotion.

If you've agreed to a TV interview about a controversial subject, talk with the reporter ahead of time to determine what he or she is building the story around. Better yet, if you are not familiar with the reporter, do some research and make sure you know what the interview is about before the camera rolls. The more you know, the better the piece.

Nor do you want to be caught off guard about an unrelated area or subject beyond the planned interview or your expertise. Someone who owns a sporting goods store may not be prepared to weigh in on the cost of gun violence or whether there should be a limit on the number of guns people are allowed to own. That doesn't mean you shouldn't be prepared for such a question, even if to say it's beyond what you're prepared to comment about.

If asked to comment on a competitor, be kind. Avoid criticizing others. If you're asked what separates you from others who do what you do, it's better to highlight the positive aspects of your services than to make negative inferences about others.

For instance, if asked why your products are better than others, don't suggest your competitors are not as good as you. Rather, say something like, "there are a lot of good, competent folks out there. Our goal is to combine top shelf products with absolutely outstanding service. We've got a lot of customer testimonials on our website at www._____ and at our store that underscore that."

You'll not only deliver your message but will also come across as a nice person to do business with.

2

Attitude

A personal note ... and a challenge

"There is nothing more dreadful than the habit of doubt. Doubt separates people. It is a poison that disintegrates friendships and breaks up pleasant relations. It is a thorn that irritates and hurts; it is a sword that kills."

Buddha, philosopher, religious leader

I thought about putting this note in the closing paragraphs because it deals with perception rather than tactics. But the fact is, how we are seen by others has a significant impact on how they interact with us. Interpersonal interaction is the most powerful component of public relations.

The most important of all is continual networking – purposefully meeting and contacting people on a never ending basis. Dave Tiberi, a long-time friend who is a former world champion boxer, runs a successful video production business in northern Delaware. He operates from a small shop in a small town, but he handles a broad range of businesses, including large corporations. (See www.tntvideo.com.)

Dave's successful because he applies the same work ethic to his business that he did when he trained for the ring. Of the 10 hour days he spends at his shop, at least six are on the phone making cold calls and follow up calls. In addition to first-class work, his success is in large part due to persistence

9

mixed with a large dose of good-natured humor that grabs people. Dave's customers never know when he's having a bad day.

Be ready to tell a stranger about your business in a concise, easy to understand way without boring or confusing him or her. The same applies to written messages. Always be ready to forward a description of what you do to anyone who asks. It's like keeping your resume updated.

Always have a verbal "one-minute commercial" ready for prospects. Practice it so it flows with natural enthusiasm but isn't rushed. It's also called an elevator pitch because you should be able to substantially relate what you do in the time it takes to ride with someone in an elevator. Avoid saying "I" (the 'perpendicular pronoun,' as a former mentor called it) as much as possible. It sounds like bragging. "What our team can do for you," or "we aim to please," sounds more professional and reassuring than a one-person show.

We are a nation of specialists. We hold expertise built on learning and doing our jobs. Years before The History Channel began explaining how Modern Marvels have changed our lives an accomplished friend expressed his ignorance about life in general. I was confused. He explained that the simple candy bar he was enjoying was a mystery. How was it made? How was it packaged? How was it shipped to the store so it would arrive in perfect condition? I had to admit I didn't know.

By the same token, how does Joe the local mechanic know how to work on computerized vehicles? How do local plumbers, electricians, heating and air conditioning specialists know how to fix our ever more sophisticated equipment? Could a walk-on with no experience do your job? Absolutely not! Feel good about yourself.

Professional expertise applies to all career paths. When I was a 17-year-old recruit, one of my barracks roommates convinced me, against my better judgment I might add, to go in halfers on a $15 do-it-yourself haircut kit from the Base Exchange. He kept talking about how fast we'd get our investment back by not having to go to the base barber shop. My grandfather, a retired coal miner from Centralia, Pa., had been a barber and even though I knew he didn't learn his trade from a booklet, I reluctantly went along. It turned out to be a bad mistake but a good learning experience.

I cut my buddy's hair first, with the instruction booklet in one hand and the clippers in the other. The book emphasized to "cut gradually." After 20 minutes of gradually cutting hair from the nape of his neck to nearly even with the top of his ears, I was grateful we didn't have a second mirror so he could check out my work.

Then it was my turn.

After he finished he asked if his hair looked as bad as mine. That's when we dropped all pretenses and laughed at what we'd done to one another. We went to different barber shops to have the damage repaired and returned with very short hair cuts. We shared comments the pros had made. My roomie's barber, in a mercifully low voice, commented that his wife was not a very good barber. Mine whispered he knew a "home job" when he saw one.

We sold the kit for $5 to some guy from Tennessee down the hall.

My point is take pride in what you do. It will show to everyone you deal with.

The Challenge

Here's the challenge. We all like being around positive people. Books have been written about the benefits of a positive outlook. We all know someone everyone likes to be around.

There's even a magazine called *POSITIVE THINKING Attitude is Everything*. Its philosophy is to "support a lifestyle brand appealing to people who know that their outlook on life determines the quality of their life, and that a great attitude ... is something that must be developed and maintained in a variety of dynamic, personally fulfilling and downright enjoyable ways. Positive Thinking permeates every major life area—work, family, friendships, community, health, spirit; it encompasses mind, body and soul. Above all, *Positive Thinking* celebrates the daily joys of life."

Thank God it's Friday…

While subscribing to a magazine won't necessarily improve someone's outlook, the fact is how others perceive us is based on how we portray ourselves to them. It's why politicians kiss babies and corporations sponsor public service efforts. Think about it. When someone asks how you're doing don't say, "I'm surviving," or "hanging in there," or "thank God it's Friday." Rather, let everyone know you're happy to have the opportunity to be doing what you do.

How about, "I'm doing great," or "couldn't be better!" or to borrow from radio financial guru Dave Ramsey, "better than I deserve!" Or maybe even, "business is outstanding because of so many repeat customers!" Sounds corny, but it conveys a positive message and confidence.

Try it. You'll find it's more of a challenge than you may think after years of repeating trite, meaningless phrases. Any coach will confirm the benefits of a positive, can-do attitude in our personal and professional lives. A positive attitude is a key component of public relations.

Dress to impress

"Since we cannot change reality, let us change the eyes which see reality."

Nikos Kazantzakis, Greek writer and philosopher

Many celebrities make it a point to dress down for interviews. They want to emphasize their commonality with the rest of us. That's fine for them because their fame has already been established and no one is judging them by their attire anyway.

For the rest of us, however, first impressions do matter. Dress appropriately for every interview, even those on radio. Why on radio? Because the most important person there will be the host. He or she will set the tenor of the interview.

Coming to an interview in work clothes or laid back clothing won't command as much respect as a person who appears in a suit or dress. Of course, if you're being interviewed for a how-to garden or auto repair program, jeans or coveralls would be appropriate.

Continue to impress your host after the interview by sending a short thank you for the courtesy. The same applies to print media. People who remember to thank others stand out.

Visuals

"Effective communication is 20% what you know and 80% how you feel about what you know."

Jim Rohn, author and motivational speaker

Put in another context, as much as 93 percent of the message in a TV interview is visual, according to body language expert Janine Driver, who says that nonverbal communication accounts for 93 percent of communication. See www.lyintamer.com.

Similarly, Patti Wood, one of the world's leading experts in nonverbal communication, says that visual communication is 55% body language and 38% voice. Words account for only 7% of our impression on people. She says to always believe body language over voice -- and both over the actual words.

Ms. Wood studied then Presidential candidate Barack Obama's speech patterns. She noted how the rhythm of his voice works within the cadence of speech, building to a pregnant pause before he delivers his most powerful words. His voice tells you what you should be feeling. The words don't matter, according to her.

She says women's voices affect the emotional parts of a man's brain. That's why men think women are more emotional. The higher the pitch or shrillness in a woman's voice, the lower the credibility she projects. Consider the close scrutiny the media placed on Senator Hillary Clinton and Gov. Sara Palin. The same scrutiny is unfairly applied to women candidates who cry or show emotion.

Interestingly, Wood contends that because of technology, we spend much less time in face-to-face interaction making it more difficult to pick up body language when we do speak to people. Consider how crucial this skill is to negotiators.

A well-documented, historic example of the effect of nonverbal communication that some think cost Richard Nixon the presidency took place September 26, 1960, in the first-ever televised presidential debate between Sen. John F. Kennedy and Vice President Richard M. Nixon.

Seventy million viewers tuned in – an impressive number, even by today's standards – to hear both men define their differences. (There were actually four televised debates but the first is regularly cited by communication scholars.)

Though each man was equally articulate in representing his position in national issues, their visual contrast was dramatic. Nixon, who had spent several weeks in the hospital for a severe knee injury, was uncomfortable and 20 pounds underweight and pallid, all of which emphasized his five o'clock shadow. Worse, he refused makeup.

Kennedy, on the other hand, had just returned from campaigning in California. He was confident, tanned and rested. His natural good looks and war hero status didn't hurt either. Still, people who heard the debate on radio proclaimed Nixon the winner.

People who watched the debate on TV, however, declared Kennedy the winner by a large margin. It also exposed Kennedy to a large audience who felt more comfortable with the 43-year-old Senator who looked much younger than his five-year-older opponent. (Nixon has also served as a Naval officer in WWII but didn't have the younger man's charisma.)

At election time six percent of voters said the debate alone influenced their votes in the closest election of the century, with Kennedy receiving only 113,000 votes more than Nixon out of 68 million cast.

In 1981 a colleague and I did an interview about a contentious subject on WABC, a major New York radio station. He wore a sports coat, open collar shirt and a pair of neatly creased jeans. I chose a low-key pin-stripe business suit, white shirt, and tie. I knew I was overdressed (but in reality, you can never be overdressed for an interview).

When we entered the studio for a pre-interview introduction, the host looked up, reminded me this wasn't TV and jokingly asked who I dressed up for. Without skipping a beat, I said, "you." He was speechless for a few seconds then smiled and shifted the conversation to other things. But the impression had been made. The program was an hour-long talk and call in show. Being the professional he was he asked the critical questions we expected, but he also treated me with the utmost respect and even took my side with argumentative callers.

Obviously, visual cues are much more important on TV. Unless you're doing an impromptu on camera interview representing your business:

- Dress as you would for a job interview because in a sense that's what it is.
- Look at the reporter, not the camera.
- Don't squint, especially if you've got a beard. It can make you look hostile or like you're trying to hide something.
- Don't slouch to reach the microphone, let the reporter bring it up to you.
- Don't mumble or trail off on a response.
- Don't be stiff. Show appropriate emotion.
- Smile a lot.

Whether radio or TV this is your opportunity to be invited back by impressing the host and the audience with your demeanor and your subject matter knowledge.

In conjunction with your follow up thank you note, let the interviewer know you'll be happy to make yourself available for any future need.

Guests sometimes cancel at the last minute, leaving the host stranded. If you've struck a resonant chord with the host or producer you may get an unexpected call to fill the slot with your area of wisdom. Go for it, but make certain you know what angle the host intends to pursue.

When you're doing a radio interview, take note cards with bulleted points, both for the interviewer and yourself. It will go a long way toward keeping you and your host on track, especially when one of you gets off track exploring an interesting point or story. The same note card idea also applies to a TV interview.

During newscasts the host is reading from a teleprompter, but for an in studio session, he or she will be using small, easily-concealed notes to keep on track and so should you.

Remember to keep the conversation friendly at all times. Thank the host for asking questions that allow you to explain your points more fully.

And again, remember to always thank your host for having you as a guest at the end of the interview, even if it was about a contentious subject -- <u>especially</u> if it was about a contentious subject. Always look like the good guy.

3

Internal communication

Write a mission statement – and live by it

One of the first steps in carving out a niche is writing a mission statement, posting it for all to see, and living by it.

Mission statements define who are and how we operate. Every business has a reason for its existence. It may start as a source of income but soon take on other aspects and attributes.

Successful businesses are run by people who like what they're doing, are good at it, and have developed a following built on reputation. Reputation is built on trust and trust is built on sustained superior performance. Most successful people like doing what they do and how it makes them feel.

A mission statement should be no more than a sentence or two that immediately comes to mind and can be repeated verbatim. It should serve as a compass for you and especially for your employees, who will only be as dedicated and loyal to your business as you are.

It can be reflected in a company slogan. Consider "we try harder," the Avis slogan that focuses on providing good, clean cars at reasonable rates. Similarly, "get the Midas touch," combined with a logo of a yellow muffler makes people think not of gold, but of "Midasizing" a noisy car.

Corporations have spent tens of millions developing slogans and logos, because they create a positive mental image that people associate with the business. (A logo is a symbol or graphic representation while a slogan is a spoken or written phrase.) Strive to create an image that works for your business.

While logos and even business strategies may change over time, the key is consistency and predictability in dealing with others. Changes in business practices should be announced well in advance and in multiple ways. There should be no surprises in how you do business. This also applies to your employees who should be communicated with on an ongoing basis and asked for feedback on company decisions whenever possible. Doing so will smooth the way for tough decisions like cutbacks and layoffs.

Customer feedback

"You can either take action or you can hang back and hope for a miracle. Miracles are great, but they are so unpredictable."

Peter Drucker, management consultant and author

Ask new customers how they found you, whether through the Internet, a recommendation, your sign, a story, or advertising.

Do you ever ask your existing customers or clients how you can better serve them? Businesses depend on satisfying customers but if you have no mechanism to determine if you're doing a good job, you may find yourself losing business to the competition. Make certain your key selling messages and measurements align.

Don't wait until there's a problem, an angry call, or even until your regular customers stop coming by. Proactively solicit comments and suggestions. You may need to update your products or services and not even be aware of it. Remember, needs change, particularly if your business specializes in technology-related products or services.

It doesn't hurt to ask your customers what they think you do best. Or how you compare to the competition. <u>It's not what you think that counts but what you're customers believe you're doing for them</u> in bringing in and retaining their business.

As a small business, you have an advantage over large corporations in that you have the ability to change course quickly to keep your customers pleased. You could use a Likkert scale, gauging level of satisfaction from 1 to 5, or create your own categories like – highly pleased, somewhat pleased, neutral, somewhat displeased, highly displeased.

Next time you do a mailer, include a brief survey with a self-addressed stamped envelope or a response e-mail address. If you don't do mailers send a thank you note to your customers along with the survey. Invite e-mail responses. Offer respondents the opportunity to win a prize through a random drawing. Ask what additional services they would like you to offer. You may be surprised at the ideas or comments you receive.

Your survey might include questions asking about the quality of your products and service; friendliness of your staff; follow up; whether your customers will continue to do business with you or recommend you to a friend; or other issues specifically relevant to your situation. Consider making an anonymous response possible for those who might be fearful of offending you.

If you incorporate customer or employee feedback to make changes, report those changes in your next communication. Let respondents know you're not only listening but acting on what customers want and need. This also gives you cover to make the changes, especially during tough times.

Here's a simple survey created for a local restaurant.

Dear Customer,
Thank you for visiting us. We truly appreciate your patronage.

To better serve you we ask that you complete the following anonymous survey and place it in the feedback box in the foyer on your way out.

Please rate the following by circling the appropriate number below:
1 = outstanding 2 = good 3 = neutral 4 = fair 5 = unsatisfactory

Restaurant Cleanliness	Atmosphere	Comfort
1 2 3 4 5	1 2 3 4 5	1 2 3 4 5

Wait Staff Promptness	Accuracy	Courtesy
1 2 3 4	1 2 3 4 5	1 2 3 4 5

Food

Quality	Taste	Presentation
1 2 3 4 5	1 2 3 4 5	1 2 3 4 5

Menu Selection	Pricing
1 2 3 4 5	1 2 3 4 5

Overall Rating

1 2 3 4 5

Do you plan to return?   Yes   No

Would you recommend us to family and friends? Yes No

What improvements could we make to any of the areas above or others? Continue on back if necessary. Any and all feedback from our valued customers is important to us. Thank you!

Some businesses hire a 3rd party to do telephone surveys. Always acknowledge feedback even if it's negative. Customers who bring negatives to your attention may be providing more valuable information than those who are happy with you. They will be even more surprised when you thank them for their feedback.

Courtesy and follow up are never out of style

"Those you have followed passionately, gladly, zealously have made you feel like somebody. It wasn't merely because they had the job or the power -- they somehow made you feel terrific to be around them."

Irwin Federman, venture capitalist, author

Many small businesses lose the customers or clients they worked so hard to gain by forgetting that winning a customer is only the start of a long term cultivation and retention process. Very simply, they forget to service the client they worked so hard to take away from their competitors. Everyone needs to feel appreciated, especially during the honeymoon period.

Have you ever walked out of a store because the salesperson was ignoring you, or worse, was rude? Have you even been offended when a manager didn't return your call or get caught up in a phone loop that transferred you from one computer to another? Prospects and customers have little tolerance for that kind of non-service.

"There's a tremendous culture and value gap," says William Withers, a communications professor at Wartburg College in Iowa, who along with colleague Patrick Langan, has spent years studying customer service. Withers was referring to the difference in expectations in service between baby boomers and Gen Xers, according to Philadelphia Inquirer reporter Jeff Gammage (Wilmington Delaware News Journal 12/24/07).

Another way of keeping customers close is the after-service call. Most auto dealers follow up with a phone call from the service desk or an e-mail both thanking the customer for the business and asking for feedback.

By 2010, Withers predicted boomers will constitute nearly 50 percent of the population and control about 65 percent of the disposal income. They were raised during an era when department stores were well staffed by salespeople who politely asked how they could help. No one was expected to wait while the salesperson finished a private conversation on a cell phone.

"They're clueless," says 55-year-old Franni Segal, a travel agent with a retailing degree quoted in the same article. "They're more interested in talking to their friends. They have no incentive to make the sale." Withers blames the service gap partly on 78 percent of employers who lack the time and money to train workers.

An acquaintance who at 60 is about 20 years older than the average auto salesman, was hired away from a competing dealer because the owner wanted him to train the rest of the team how to maintain a positive attitude toward customers. He told him he didn't care if he sold any cars, he just wanted to establish an enthusiastic tone in his sales force. Common traits among successful salespeople are friendliness and enthusiasm.

Likely adding to the mess is that some large retail stores have eliminated commission, forcing their sales force to rely solely on hourly pay with little incentive to provide anything more than mediocre service. While commission doesn't apply to salaried service techs, the importance of good customer relations is paramount, especially if your employees, like on-the-road service technicians, are not normally observed.

As a one-time commercial insurance representative, I know that because of lawsuits, some commercial insurers require employers to conduct background checks on new employees and to provide training to avoid harassment and other illegal behavior toward customers and fellow employees.

Doing the right thing is important to public relations but so is avoiding negative behaviors. Make certain your employees know it is against company policy to do, say, or pass along anything you wouldn't want published in your business's name in the local newspaper. The image they project while on your time clock is yours, whether it's one of outstanding service, or involves racist, sexist, or offensive language or speeding down the road in company vehicles.

Tracking your ads for results

Deciding where to advertise and how much to spend is only the start of the process. Unless you believe in blind luck, you've got to measure results by tracking responses. Put another way, did your ad or campaign work to increase your business or just create an income stream for your ad rep?

The simplest way to track an ad's effectiveness is to ask new customers how they found out about you. But be prepared to record the results for later analysis. In other words, if your front desk people only record responses relating to a new advertisement you may miss other, more significant and unexpected responses, like favorable pricing, word-of-mouth, new products, or an appealing showroom.

One way to track ads used in multiple media outlets is to assign key code numbers. For instance, if you advertise a coupon special on widgets in several publications or through a direct mail campaign, assign a unique code to each medium. In the corner of the print ad you could use H-1(1-7) for Herald News, January 1 to 7, and change the letter to C for a Courier ad.

You should also have multiple versions of your domain name that point to your designated landing page on your business website. Domain names are cheap, generally about $10 per year. Grab names that logically say what you do, then buy close variations of it to prevent a competitor from siphoning off some of your business.

Direct mail advertising can be identified by the last digits of zip codes incorporated into the ad, corresponding to where it was mailed. Similarly, electronic ads could use a special name or phone number for tracking purposes. Ever hear a celebrity say, "just tell them _____ sent you for an additional discount"?

The same applies to snail mail or email direct response ads that use a special offer or box number. Your website administrator can also offer solutions to differentiate responses.

The key is not only to measure the number of leads you get but also to determine where your advertising money is best spent to generate actual business.

Post sale strategy

"Wishful thinking is not a strategy that will work in this environment."

Margie Johnson, business consultant

When you land a good contract or secure a sizable sale, a thank you note or call should be a part of your post sale checklist. It shows the customer you appreciate her business and want to keep it. Friendly and consistent follow up service is mandatory in building customer loyalty.

Find out why customers chose you and what it will take to keep their business even when the competition undercuts your prices – because sooner or later they will. One very good way to keep your clients is to regularly educate them about what you do and why it benefits them to follow your advice. Give them outstanding service when they are not expecting it, such as calling when a product has been updated or should be replaced. Or a check-in, "I-was-wondering-how-you're-doing" contact.

An A+ rated commercial insurance company I worked for required me to visit each client four times a year. Each visit had to do with providing proactive service rather than waiting for the client to come to me for help -- or worse, to my competition. Being proactive with clients and prospects also paves the way for additional sales if you plan properly.

Train and retrain your employees to always be professional, even with a customer who adamantly believes he has been taken advantage of, especially when you believe you are not going to be able to satisfy him. If you think a customer or client is displeased it's much better to clear the air than to ignore it or assume it will blow over. It's better to part company with a mere difference of opinion than an angry former customer who's out to tell everyone how bad you are. TV's finger-jabbing lawyers make a living reminding people why they should be angry at anyone who might even have thought about taking advantage of them.

That's not to say there are no limits to the customer-is-always-right, but your employees should occasionally be reminded that even though you write their paychecks, it's the customer who makes it good.

Everyone has had the occasional client or customer whom they've had to suggest would be better served elsewhere. But even in those situations keep your cool because they may end up coming back to you if they believe there's no penalty for doing so. That said, don't forget to acknowledge your employees when they do outstanding work in client cultivation and retention. Stand behind them when you have reason to believe they're being abused by difficult customers or vendors.

An outstanding graphic artist who once worked for me confided that a rep of one of the printing shops we regularly used had become verbally abusive toward her over a period of several months. She asked if it was ok to use another, equally competent but slightly more expensive printer. She was worried I'd be upset for bringing it to my attention. My only question was why she hadn't already fired him, a matter she quickly resolved.

Not long after I opened my public relations practice my sister gave me a small, framed definition: *"Irish diplomacy: The ability to tell a man to go to hell in such a way that he'll look forward to the trip."* It's come in handy more than once.

4

External Communication

Using multiple approaches for visibility and credibility

Consider chamber of commerce membership a budgeted cost of doing business. The chamber exists to serve its members. They are an invaluable source of contacts and leads, and advocate for the interests of their members. But they work best when members engage with them.

Dues generally run between $100 to $300, annually depending on the size of the business. Some have monthly mixers that provide a wonderful opportunity for cross pollination with other business owners. Other services often include things like free business advice through pairing retired executives with new business owners. It's a very worthwhile, tax deductible investment in yourself as well as your business. Consider this organization your best sounding board and learning laboratory.

Organizations dedicated to business owners present a great opportunity to meet like minded entrepreneurs, some of whom may become clients and referral sources. Exchanging leads is always a good idea and creates bonds between and among the business community. Many years ago in basic military training I was taught to "cooperate and graduate." That advice has proven useful over a lifetime.

Most chambers have newsletters and will publish a submitted story and photo when a new business joins. Some will come out to a ribbon cutting if asked. This is free publicity so take advantage of it. They are also good conduits for business-to-business advertising.

Chambers generally sponsor seasonal trade shows, usually over a weekend at a mall or other public location.

Some suggestions:

- Rent a booth to display your business.
- Make time to regularly meet and interact with other business owners.
- Suggest partnerships through mutual referrals.
- Offer a discount.
- Pair up with other businesses to offer a promotion package.
- Host a chamber mixer or open house at your business. Always have a supply of business cards with you, whether on a business call or socializing. And make certain to ask other people for theirs so you may include them on your master list of contacts.
- Write an article for your chamber newsletter. Let others know how they can save money, time or effort by providing tips in your area of expertise. If you don't write well, there are plenty of people available to help you.

Entrepreneurs achieve success by being proactive in helping people and a grateful community will further enhance an organization's prosperity. Every town has service clubs like Rotary, Lions, Elks, Moose, Soroptimist, and Kiwanis, among others. Choose the one that best suits your needs. But avoid joining strictly to promote your business or you'll soon become someone to avoid.

On the other hand, don't become the person who never says "no" to requests for help on every club project, or even worse, one who is expected to give his or her product or expertise away to every charitable or non-profit group that asks. When something is given free, people tend to believe the price defines its worth. Like life, keep things in balance. And smile a lot.

There are also a growing number of business to business networking clubs. These organizations provide excellent opportunities to meet and exchange leads. This has the possibility of expanding your contacts exponentially. One of the oldest and largest is BNI, Business Networking International, but there are smaller, community-based clubs that charge no dues. To prevent internal conflicts most networking organizations only allow one of each kind of business.

Yet another method is to form a consortium of people with related skill subsets who serve similar clients and who will refer business to one another. My own business is made up of fellow professionals with proven expertise in various facets of mass communication, including PR, video production, script and speechwriting, government relations, graphics, media training, and strategic planning. Each is independent but all have been vetted for their abilities.

If you provide a service, consider hosting a free or at-cost seminar for the public. Inform the media at least two weeks in advance and let your reporter friends know about it as well. That doesn't mean they'll come, but it never hurts to keep them in the loop.

Weekend events are good for the public but not for assignment editors, who have to pay their reporters overtime. This doesn't mean you can't hand out questionnaires to your audience soliciting contact information or comments for use in a follow-up press release or future advertising.

Swap services with other professionals. This quid pro quo exchange of expertise or goods can not only save money but also introduce others to your business and broaden your network of contacts. You don't know what someone else will offer unless you ask.

How do I determine which media to use? Who are my audiences? Print advertising

Advertising can be used for direct or indirect sales, i.e., to promote a specific product or service, or to foster institutional good will, such as corporate sponsorship of educational programming.

The print ad has been with us since cavemen in Chauvet-Pont-d'Arc in today's France drew crude pictures of the animals they hunted more than 30,000 years ago. Twenty-five thousand years later, Egyptians told of the accomplishments of their leaders in hieroglyphics. In 1450, Johannes Gutenberg developed the printing press, which in 1997 Time-Life magazine declared the most important invention of the second millennium.

For better or for worse, we've progressed from there.

On a more serious note, TNS Media Intelligence, the leading provider of strategic advertising and marketing information, predicted in January 2008 that total US advertising spending for that year would be $153.7 billion. Cymfony, a TNS Media Intelligence company, tells brands and companies what people are saying about them, whether the people are bloggers, traditional journalists or even influential consumers. This helps companies identify issues and respond to the trends impacting their business.

Since the Industrial Revolution of the 19th century, merchants and other advertisers have used increasingly sophisticated print ads to entice us to notice them. Print ads are non-interactive, one-way messages whose purpose is to tell prospective customers or clients about products and services and how to obtain them.

While they bring the selling proposition to the attention of readers, newspaper ads have a one-day life span, with weekly papers faring a little better. This makes the case for a campaign of regular insertions to give people multiple opportunities to see and react to an ad as well as to build recognition and credibility for the advertiser.

Another vehicle for print ads are magazines, which may be read for months after publication, in addition to targeting special interest groups. (Based on the number of missing coupons and partial pages, I suspect the doctor's office may come second to the library for magazine reading.)

Philip W. Sawyer, of Starch Communications, a New York firm specializing in readership studies, found that ads whose headlines include a benefit and a strong visual focal point grab the reader's attention and cause them to spend more time because they address the age old question of "what's in it for me?"

A Starch Communications study on behalf of the Newspaper Association of America showed that when three-quarters of ad space was devoted to illustrations, recognition rates improved by 50 percent.

From AOL Money & Finance:
Best Ads of All Time

"A Diamond is Forever" – (1947) DeBeers most recognized advertising line of the 20th century according to Ad Age magazine.

"Have it Your Way," Burger King of the mid-70s, in response to McDonalds rigidity.

"Tastes Great, Less Filling," Miller Lite since 1974.

"A Different Kind of Company – A Different Kind of Car" Saturn – launched mid-80s to compete with Japan

"Think Small" Volkswagen, 1960s. Adage.com voted this the top ad campaign of all time.

"Ring Around the Collar," Wisk. Mid-60s. One of the most annoying commercials of all time.

"Mikey Likes It" Life Cereal 1972-84. One of the longest running campaigns in history of advertising.

"We'll Leave the Light on For You," Motel 6. mid-80s.

"We Try Harder" Avis 1962 to compete against Hertz

"When You Care Enough To Send The Very Best" Hallmark 1944, created by a salesman at a meeting.

"A Little Dab'll Do Ya," Brylcreem. 40s-50s.

Radio and TV advertising

"Between two evils, I always pick the one I never tried before"

Mae West, film star, comedienne

Because of production costs, many small business owners believe running TV ads is out of their price range. Surprisingly, advertising on the majority of cable TV stations is very inexpensive once you have your ad produced, in some cases less than $10 a spot.

There are also a growing number of home-based, first-class, videographer entrepreneurs with sophisticated equipment who can produce a professional commercial for your business with special effects formerly reserved for network spots. They've prospered because many cable TV providers don't find it profitable to produce their own commercials. These folks also tend to be experts in Internet technology and can put streaming video on your website.

Radio, on the other hand, is immediate. They are in the business of producing commercials with a variety of ideas, sound effects and talent. They will write your script, suggest a schedule targeted to your audience, and can put you on the air in the time it takes to record your spot, as early as the same day. But it is your responsibility to have a good idea of the message you want to deliver and an idea of your target audience in order to determine the length of your campaign and expected results.

Both radio and local cable television are within the price range of most small entrepreneurs. Your messages should be consistent with the theme of your print ads, and vice versa. <u>Consistency of message among mediums is important for recognition and retention</u>, particularly on limited ad budgets. Talk with your ad reps. They have a wealth of knowledge and want your ad campaign to be successful so you will become a loyal client of theirs.

Finding media addresses

Virtually everything is available on line today and the list grows exponentially each month. Use key words "media addresses" for your area and a great many links will appear. For more precise data, type in the name of your local print and electronic media outlets and their webpage will come up. Or, just buy a paper. Editors and their contact information are listed in every copy.

Then it's just a matter of contacting media outlets to pinpoint the most appropriate person. Update your list every six months. Although news organizations have a long life, reporters routinely move to other assignments, locations, or employment. Make certain you're communicating with the right person. Unlike the post office, media organizations will not return undelivered messages to you.

The first step is determining which radio and TV station(s) and other media outlets your prospective customers are most likely to watch, listen to or read.

Listen to local radio stations and their formats. Each station can provide demographic statistics on their listeners and when they listen. Additionally, listening to other ads can provide some great ideas – as will asking others what ads stand out for them. Just don't copy a competitor's format or you'll find yourself advertising for him.

Drive time -- when people are going to and coming from work -- is the most expensive time. To offset the cost marketing representatives will provide a rotating schedule that includes a mixture of times around the clock.

The least expensive buy is the ROS (run of station) package but unless you're targeting long-distance truckers or midnight-shift workers, be careful the majority of your ads don't run between 2 and 6 a.m.

Repetition is the key to making an impression on people. People have short memories so be careful of dumping a substantial portion of your advertising budget into what seems like a great idea, such as sponsoring a big event that will be forgotten when the game clock runs out.

Consistency and persistency are the keys to reaching and influencing customers. Be creative in your approach. A Small Business Administration advisor I know tells his clients to laser focus on prospects most likely to see the need for their services.

Too many startup businesses use a shotgun approach in blindly advertising to everyone, believing customers will come to them. Others don't know that messages require multiple repetitions (as many as eight) to catch the listener's or viewer's attention and underfund their advertising campaigns.

From a public relations perspective, ask yourself these questions before you design and construct your marketing pitch:

- Who are you targeting? Are you focusing on the right audience?

- Do you want to try to reach everyone a few times or a targeted group long enough to have an effect?

- What is your actual area of influence, i.e., how far do your customers travel to reach you? Why advertise across the state if 90 percent of your customers live within 15 miles of your business?

- What are you offering that will cause a prospective customer to respond?

- What separates you from competitors offering similar products or service? Is it your outstanding service, length of time in business, location, prices, or reputation? Everyone is unique. Emphasize what makes you special, but most important, <u>how that benefits your customers</u>.

- What is the best way to reach your audience?

- What is/are your most important message(s)? Simplicity of message is essential for acceptance and retention.

Lisa Fortini-Campbell, Ph.D., at Northwestern University's Kellogg School of Management in Evanston, Ill., and author of *Hitting the Sweet Spot: How Consumer Insights Can Inspire Better Marketing and Advertising*, recommends researching target audiences up front because too often business owners assume they know what their customers will want before doing their homework.

She points out that marketers lose focus on the fact that people persuade themselves based on information provided to them. Her book provides 12 principles on consumer insight and suggests that clients and the marketing team collaborate to achieve marketing goals.

Larger companies delve more deeply into consumer research through ethnography, an offshoot of anthropology that examines people in their natural environments. It takes culture, environment, beliefs, values and interaction with others into account. It's based on the common sense premise that people react differently in their home environment than they would in a focus group or with a crowd of strangers.

In an Internet interview on April 20, 2006, Microsoft's ethnographer Tracey Lovejoy said, "In today's competitive and global market, companies are increasingly finding it necessary to deeply understand their customer and build their products accordingly. Anthropology is a discipline with a long history of studying people and understanding their lives in the contexts of their normal environments in cultures around the world."

Business or marketing research ethnography provides a holistic view of consumers in the context of their daily lives. It takes into account changing family patterns, cultural factors and social interaction patterns that affect consumer behavior. Again, it's why the local mom and pop corner store specializing in ethnic food continues to hold its own against megastores.

Other factors from Communication 101

Many years ago, in a freshman sociology course I learned we are subject to three basic communication filters that affect how we see things: **selective attention, selective perception, and selective retention.** Let's use a political debate as a simplified example.

Selective attention: People listen to the candidate they support, not really paying much attention to his or her opponent, except as it may relate to their own preconceived ideas.

Selective perception: Supporters are convinced their candidate won the debate, especially on issues important to them and wonder why everyone else doesn't agree.

Selective retention: People remember what their candidate said and how much of an impact it had on them, sometimes even to the point of remembering things that weren't said.

Anyone who's raised children is familiar with this process.

It shares common ground with the **reticular activating system** of our brains, which filters out information and background noise not deemed important to a given situation. It deals with two categories of information, both of which are relevant to our immediate situation and to perceived danger.

1) Information that is immediately valuable but not necessarily life threatening. Your car needs new tires and you find sudden interest in tire sale ads, or you're going to travel for the holidays and you begin intently listening to the weather channel.

2) You sense a threat. Is that 2 a.m. noise downstairs the cat or something else? A mother hears a car screeching outside and immediately checks on her children. These reactions come from a sense of danger based on not being in control of our environment.

The same process applies to our everyday lives and businesses. Offering a service or guarantee that will provide ease of mind to customers or clients can give you a leg up on your competition. Ever have a customer who heard and recalled a completely different version of the verbal guarantee you provided? Maybe the guarantee should have been in writing. Remember, it's all about your customers and what will bring them to you and keep them coming back. They want to feel protected and comfortable.

Look at your advertising as the first step in the process of making them loyal customers. Bringing them into your store to buy something should be seen as the first step in a long term relationship. Let your customers and clients know you value them and their continued trust in you.

Shaping the message

"Life is not measured by the breaths you take, but rather the moments that take your breath away."

Unknown

Public relations professionals define their audiences as "publics" or "stakeholders." We all have publics, whether professional or personal. We speak to our spouse differently than we do to our children, our parents, our in-laws, our co-workers, and employees. Our customers are no different.

Our communication with established customers will be more specific than our messages to the public at large. Our clients already know who we are and what we do. Our messages to them will be more customer-service oriented than to people we haven't yet met but want to cultivate.

Research tells us to personalize our message to prospective customers. On a larger level, many newspapers, particularly weeklies, can target advertising inserts to zip codes and neighborhoods. Advertising to specific demographic groups is the norm today. As previously noted, your communication about your business should have a consistent theme, whether verbal, print, radio or TV. Research shows that people remembers consistent messages, especially when they are received over different media. That's the power of logos and slogans that tie everything together.

A home improvement contractor should be targeting publications distributed in established neighborhoods rather than new housing developments. Similarly, a landscaping contractor would be wasting money advertising in a publication primarily distributed to condominium owners.

As obvious as that sounds, out of force of habit many businesses routinely advertise in publications that don't target their prospective customers or even conform to their advertising theme. Business owners are often deluged with calls to advertise on association phone book covers, in organizational and professional periodicals and obscure rosters that have little chance of catching anyone's eye, much less those of prospective customers.

If you have a problem saying no, ask the solicitor to send you specific demographic information in order to satisfy your business ad policy. This is guaranteed to frustrate the script-reading solicitor guilt-tripping you to support your local police, fire station, and high school athletic team. (You're better off to contribute directly to local public service organizations since all of the money goes to them.)

Message, Medium and Money

Message, Medium and **Money** are three important elements of promotion planning.

Messages must be clearly defined through research. What are the most important things you need to communicate to your audiences? Note "need" is different from "want" because you've only got several seconds to catch and keep the attention of readers, listeners, and viewers. Putting a great message together is time-consuming but necessary so you're not just saying whatever comes to mind hoping someone will respond. You need to choose the benefits that will make your customers and prospects say, "Not only do I want that, I need it!" How many who stood in line for the rollout of the iPhone really needed a $500 multi-function computer incorporated into their phones?

Mediums that will be most effective in getting your message out are the next part of the equation. Tailoring your messages will force you to define to whom you want to sell your products or services. Knowing who your targeted audiences are makes it easier to determine where to place your advertisements, send your press releases, and direct your publicity. Mediums also include influential people who can help you get the word out through word of mouth and personal endorsements.

Money, to paraphrase a well-known and often misquoted bible verse, is really the root of all excellence when it comes to business. Cash flow determines whether businesses succeed. It is why people go into business in the first place. But it is also finite and when it comes to advertising must be used efficiently and, most of all, effectively. Always consider co-op advertising possibilities where a product manufacturer or even a related business agrees to share promotion costs.

Emotional triggers

"Dahling, I've got to tell you something, and I don't say this to everybody. You look mahvelous! Absolutely mahvelous! It's not how you feel, it's how you look!"

Billy Crystal as Fernando on Saturday Night Live

Marshall McLuhan (1911-1980), the man who coined the term "global village" and the phrase "the medium is the message," was an early expert on the effect of the media on human interaction. He taught us that just by virtue of being on TV or in the media, the subject gained importance and was itself changed, similar to the notion that it's impossible to put one's foot in the same stream twice. But one can also argue that our overexposure to media has moderated its effect.

More recently, Frank Luntz, political consultant and author of the best selling book, "Words that Work," gained national exposure by graphing real time audience reaction to political candidates during debates.

"We decide based on how people look; we decide based on how people sound; we decide based on how people are dressed. We decide based on their passion. If I respond to you quietly, the viewer at home is going to have a different reaction than if I respond to you with emotion and with passion and I wave my arms around. But that's how we make up our minds," he said in an interview with PBS Frontline, posted on the Internet.

Luntz added that emotion easily overrides intellect. "Eighty percent of our life is emotion, and only 20 percent is intellect. I am much more interested in how you feel than how you think. I can change how you think, but how you feel is something deeper and stronger, and it's something that's inside you. How you think is on the outside, how you feel is on the inside, so that's what I need to understand."

Award-winning videographer Jason Gleockler from Felton, Delaware, firmly believes the message IS the message. His strength is in bringing the essence of his client's business to the TV screen by emphasizing the touchstones and emotional aspects of what is being offered versus the traditional eye candy of good looking models to sell everything from cars, to clothing, to perfume.

Upon accepting a client he learns what there is to know and thinks in terms of how they could be positioned to cut through the clutter and grab the viewer's attention. "This is what makes for authenticity and believability," he says.

Advertisements that trigger an emotional response can hold the attention of an audience and leave them with a warm and cozy feeling about the company, product or service.

The fact is, regardless of country of origin or political system, we all share the human condition. The "warm fuzzies" of family, courage, and belief in the future strike a resonant cord is all of us. If wrapped in the proper visuals, themes and music, these feelings can easily translate into sales.

Think about the commercials that have touched you or were funny enough that you couldn't wait to tell others about them. Consider the emotion evoked when Whitney Houston's "One moment in time," played as Olympic athletes were shown competing in slo-mo, then accepting their medals on the stand.

On the humorous side, remember Clara Peller as the old woman asking fast food restaurants "Where's the beef?" Her question evoked more than humor. Like the line in the movie "Jerry McGuire," when athlete Cuba Gooding Jr., told his agent, played by Tom Cruise to "Show me the money!,"

Clara represented a basic question we've all asked about life and became a classic.

The key, however, is to successfully tie your commercial message into the emotional one, otherwise you'll end up sponsoring a great message that will make people cry, laugh and talk about it – but won't recall a thing about the product.

We love stories of personal courage and commitment and those who appreciate and support great values. Consider sponsoring an event or making a contribution to a local veterans' group, or a community service agency, or a volunteer organization. Businesses that sponsor scholarships for needy students can create long term good will.

The point is, plan your advertising, your message, and your budget and stick with them until they show results or a need to retool. Consider advertising as a well-planned investment, rather than a contribution to your local charity or an ongoing commitment to your local ad rep. Use a rifle rather than a shotgun approach to advertising. It will not only save you money, but also make it easier to determine what worked best.

In addition to paid advertising, small businesses should always employ a healthy portion of creative imagination.

Guerilla Marketing, a groundbreaking 1984 book by Jan Conrad Levinson, is based on continually brainstorming about ways to connect with people in unusual and cost effective ways. It relies on energy and imagination to supplement paid advertising. It is often, in-your-face, local tactics that grabs people's attention. It includes people with sandwich boards, sign twirling, costumed characters advertising a sale or a new business, an impromptu sale based around an event, or some other eye-catching scheme designed to grab people's attention.

Be aggressive but be sensible in your tactics. Sometime unconventional tactics go awry. In January 2007, when police were notified about small, battery operated devices placed around Boston and surrounding cities, they notified bomb squads. After areas of the cities were closed for several hours, the devices were determined to be LED placards with cartoon images promoting an animated film by Cartoon Network.

The network reportedly paid $1,000,000 in reimbursement to the Massachusetts Port Authority, Highway Department, State Police, and the U.S. Coast Guard and another $1,000,000 in goodwill payments to the Department of Homeland Security.

The SWOT Analysis

Part of determining what your business message should be is making a determination about the circumstances in which your business operates.

Wikipedia puts it succinctly: "**SWOT Analysis** is a strategic planning tool used to evaluate the **S**trengths, **W**eaknesses, **O**pportunities, and **T**hreats involved in a project or in a business venture. It involves specifying the objective of the business venture or project and identifying the internal and external factors that are favorable and unfavorable to achieving that objective. The technique is credited to Albert Humphrey, who led a research project at Stanford University in the 1960s and 1970s using data from Fortune 500 companies."

A simple SWOT analysis for a landscaping company might look like the following example. It could be used to justify investing in growth in a new location or for examining alternative ways to expand the business's area of operation from its present location.

Strengths	Weaknesses	Opportunities	Threats
Well known throughout the region for quality and fair prices.	Lack of qualified workers to complete jobs on time.	New markets within a well defined growth niche.	Multi-state conglomerate may move into area.
Experience in all type landscaping from private to commercial locations.	Located about 35 miles from rapidly growing areas of new development.	Larger markets available if company could expand to a satellite location.	Cost of advertising in a new, upscale market area is prohibitive.
Owns its own plant and tree nursery and can control expenses.	Lack of marketing budget to advertise in new market areas.	Has capacity to sell plants to competitors.	Inability to easily reach new market area.

In reference to the matrix, an established business at its well-maintained roadside location, awards for public service, and years of expertise are proud features of the enterprise. But its easily accessible location, discount prices and broad selection based on an in-house nursery and tree farm are the <u>benefits that bring shoppers</u> to them.

What's missing in the example is the detailed demographics, like age, socio-economics, ethnicity, spending patterns, and type of housing and building patterns crucial to decision making in this type of business. Once everything is factored in, a determination can be made whether there are enough new potential customers to justify a business expansion.

People buy benefits, not features. Customers are fickle. They all listen to WIFM – What's In it For Me. That you've been in business for 50 years may be a bragging point on your family's business acumen, but to many it's only secondary to what's on sale and, as indicated in the matrix, what's within a reasonable driving distance.

While the SWOT is really related to the question of whether to expand to a satellite location within easy reach of new markets, the business owner should also consider more creative ways to advertise to prospective customers outside his area of dominant influence. Doing so could save the expense of opening a satellite location.

Letting people know about your business

"Never doubt that a small group of thoughtful, committed people can change the world. Indeed, it is the only thing that ever has."

Margaret Mead, cultural anthropologist, author

Think about the service providers you patronize. What stands out about them? Is it their outstanding advertisements or could it be their personalities, willingness to please, product, or service that made a positive impression on you?

Likewise, know who you're serving and who you want to serve. Put yourself in the position of your customers. What do they want, expect and deserve from you?

Immerse yourself in your specialty. Study your target industry and audience. Be seen as the expert who knows her stuff. Go public with your knowledge through letters to the editor, solicited interviews, flyers and public forums. People will come to you.

Reach out to people who might benefit from what you offer whether directly or indirectly. One of the articles of faith in marketing is that people lead to other people.

Cultivate influential people and groups. This is a big one. In the #1 national best seller, *"The Tipping Point, How Little Things Can Make a Big Difference,"* Malcolm Gladwell underscores the power of "connectors," who influence others.

Some people, because of their notoriety, visibility, or personality literally know hundreds or even thousands of people. Directly and indirectly they influence exponential number of people by what they do, the products they use, what they wear, and what they say. This is the great power of celebrity endorsement. Think about this. If Oprah would endorse this book, I'd never have to work again!

But not all connectors are famous in the sense of immediate face or name recognition. Some hold influential positions in organizations that affect others, for instance, a bank president, a hospital administrator, an elected official, a TV commentator, a newspaper editor, a cultural affairs organizer, or even a social action leader. These movers are usually familiar with other decision makers and connectors, and present an untapped resource.

Many of these same folks are engaged in multiple levels of activity. They possess the ability to introduce people to other people on a grand scale. And the people they connect with remember them and drop their names to others in ever deeper matrixes. Even people who have never met them often believe they know them. When a connector speaks, people listen.

The point is, by treating everyone as though they are very important, it's a sure bet when you unknowingly encounter someone who can boost your chances of success, you'll be prepared for the opportunities they bring.

Or better yet, increase your chance of meeting a connector by becoming one yourself. Make it a point to introduce yourself to people at social events and business mixers. Act as though you're running for office and every hand you shake is a potential vote for you as a connector. As any political candidate will tell you, the most difficult hand to shake is the first one and practice makes perfect.

Do more than meet expectations. Exceed them. Stretch occasionally. A heating and air conditioning contractor who winterizes vacation homes can proactively contact customers who may have forgotten to call him. He can also offer energy saving tips to customers as seasons change. Such things may seem small, but to customers used to receiving nothing but bills and solicitations from businesses, it stands out.

An electrician friend makes it a point to let his customers know that if an emergency happens on a holiday they should not hesitate to call him. He earned the life-long loyalty of a large family several years ago when he made an emergency call on Christmas day. Their electricity was shut off by the fire department after an overloaded circuit caused a small fire as they were preparing a family dinner.

He not only repaired the circuit but also retrieved the meter head from the fire marshal and turned the power back on. The service call was local and only involved him so when he was asked how much it was going to cost, he wished them a Merry Christmas. This man never wants for work. One can only imagine how many references resulted from this kindness.

Another man who ran a small used car business in a poorer residential area of a small town always made it a point to be friendly with his neighbors. He even made emergency repairs to their autos at cost. His neighbors reciprocated by keeping an eye on his unfenced property after business hours.

Remember your business cards represent you. Don't buy the cheapest stock or artwork you can find. Absolutely avoid the do-it-yourself cards some print out on their computer programs. Cards should be of stiff stock and contain your logo and/or slogan, address, phone(s), fax, and website or e-mail address. Give people multiple ways to reach you but avoid including too much information or type that's hard to read by myopic baby boomers. Know your target audience.

I've told my communication students to have business cards available throughout their college experience. They can be ordered inexpensively from a number of Internet printers and can be routinely changed at minimal cost during internships as education progresses. I've even had cards created at www. Vistaprint.com that feature the cover of this book to hand out to influencers.

Other methods

Once someone has made an initial contact with you it's important to follow up with him or her. How many times have you seen something in an ad you intended to follow up on but found an obstacle in the way that discouraged you? The phone line might have been busy, the website wasn't available or your call wasn't returned.

The point is you've got to think of your advertising that way. Very few customers or clients close the deal on first contact. They want to be reassured about you through multiple contacts. That's why you should view self-promotion as an ongoing priority, whether in occasional letters to the editor, seasonal seminars, speaking engagements, or even paid advertising. Messages should include a call to action.

Even someone in immediate need of a set of tires or a refrigerator is still going to look for the shop he believes will give him the best deal or at least provide the best advice. But you also want customers and prospects who don't have an immediate need to respond to your sales or clearance events because they trust you.

The same applies to up selling or crossing selling additional products to customers. Establishing trust makes a sale much easier. Someone buying tires is more likely to understand the wisdom of having a wheel alignment done just as a customer having an obsolete heater or air conditioner serviced is likely to be interested in buying a new unit if shown sufficient reason to do so.

By keeping track of your customers and their needs and sending out reminder notices and information that could help them, you'll increase sales and earn their appreciation. This is why doctors, dentists, and other health care professionals send out reminder notices and make follow up calls. It's a matter of maintaining relationships you've already established and keeping trust you've already earned.

Consider cross marketing with another business that sells things compatible with your product or service. In the previously mentioned example of the tire store, if the business didn't include wheel alignment equipment, they might offer a 20 percent off coupon to a related garage that does. The garage would offer a similar coupon for tires at the first shop with both businesses benefiting from the relationship. You can also benefit from shared prospect lists.

The fact is, during tough economic times, businesses selling similar products or services that might not have been a threat to one another when ready cash and credit was available are now often in direct competition, sometimes for survival.

Don't assume only hometown media will be interested in following up with you. Though editors primarily look for local relevancy, they also look for the offbeat. If you've got a unique way of doing something it doesn't hurt to let regional media know about it.

National stories about people in an off-the-beaten-path town usually start with a local or regional affiliate and spread. For many years the late Charles Kuralt specialized in telling human interest stories about Joe and Sally Sixpack from across the country. Charles Osgood continued that tradition on CBS every Sunday morning.

Following is a sample media contact list that includes local and regional media. Depending on the release, you may want to limit the distribution to local outlets. For instance, a new sales rep coming aboard your company would likely not be of interest to regional media.

Use good judgment and don't send material to specialized media or trade publications you know don't carry the kind of information you're offering. It not only wastes your time but you risk being seen as a rookie who doesn't understand the media.

The point is to keep a regular, balanced flow of relevant information going out to your internal and external stakeholders. Remember, the equation: visibility equals credibility.

Keeping records

Media List

Media List: Last Updated: _____

Story Idea Pitched _____ Date: _____

Name	Phone/Fax	Address	E-mail
Print Media			
Home Gazette	258-1213/14	3233 Elm St.	JohnB@Gaz.com
Daily Banner	258-1259/60	1560 Main St.	MaryR@Banner.com
Radio			
WABX 100.5FM	236-9034/37	" "	JensenR@abx.com
WNKR 1040AM	236-4597/65	" "	BoHarsen@nkr.com
TV			
WABC CH 6	235-8792/93	" " "	" " "
WNBC CH10	235-2947/48	" " "	" " "

The list can also serve as a record of all clips and electronic interviews in your file. This will keep you from pitching the same story twice. For instance, if you send a release about a new employee, list the person's name up top, date it, and put a check mark next to the mediums contacted and file it. Resulting clips can be filed with it.

Heads Up: Electronic coverage can be recorded or just noted on this record. If your boss is going to want a copy of his or her TV interview, it's much easier to record it as it is being aired than to request a copy from the station, which may charge you $50 to $100.

Outreach and Engagement

Letters to the editor can be a great source of free publicity. But because it is designed to introduce your expertise and approachability be wary of saying anything negative about your competition lest it send a negative message about you.

Being in business means having superior knowledge about a product, process or service. Use that expertise to provide helpful hints to the public at large. Better yet, call the editor of your local newspaper and ask if he or she would like an article tailored to helping readers.

The free information you provide is a low-cost teaser about what you know and will serve to establish visibility and credibility in your area. People like free advice and will pay for your expertise when they get in over their heads.

For instance, someone who sells health-related products can write about ways to eat more nutritiously, reduce cholesterol and the importance of exercise and weight control. Baby boomers, born between 1946-64, spend some $600 billion a year on health care and maintenance. That number is increasing daily and is expected to reach a trillion dollars by 2010. That's a huge amount of cash flowing into a lot of pockets.

It's why new drug stores are large buildings, almost always commanding a corner lot. They are usually mega-business chain stores that in addition to filling prescriptions, sell vitamins, supplements, household goods, and even wheelchairs and hospital supplies. Some businesses, like Sam's Club, periodically bring in health professionals to check blood pressure as a service to their customers, building good will.

As this is being written "green" contractors and businesspeople are being accorded special attention. Their opinions on construction materials, methods, and energy savings are given weight and their statements are often quoted. If you're a building contractor or sell energy related supplies, write something up for your local media on how people can reduce their energy bills.

Similarly, physical and cyber security experts command attention when they express their views, especially after stories about break-ins or crime sprees, which are always grist for the media mill. The concerns about personal and corporate identity theft have resulted in the rise of Internet security consultants. Everyone who depends on a computer fears viruses and theft of sensitive information.

Computer dealers and repair shops should hold information workshops on basic security, or at least write articles for their local papers and suggest they are willing to be interviewed on these subjects. Editors and news directors like follow ups to their stories, so if you've got a solution to a problem they've highlighted, you've got a better than average shot at being covered.

There will always be areas of specialization that draw media attention. But whatever field you're in, when it's your turn, be prepared. Keep informed about local, national and even global events. And there's nothing wrong with just pitching a story out of the blue. You may be just what local editors are looking for in a hometown connection to a broader story.

Advertising & what to spend

Although there is no hard number, a generally accepted rule of thumb is to invest at least five percent of your budget in advertising. Get the most out of your ad rep by asking the right questions.

Advertising campaigns should be driven by planning. Unless you're giving cash away on a first-come-first-served basis, don't plan to succeed based on one ad or one media outlet.

It's been said the average person needs to see or hear an ad as many as seven or eight times before it sinks in. Consider the multi-million dollar 30-second spots created for the Super Bowl each year. Some folks tune in just to watch the brilliant ideas unfold.

Roy H. Williams, author of *The Wizard of Ads*, and a number of books on award-winning ads, warns against confusing response with results by creating clever, funny and creative ads and assuming they will result in sales. "When we confuse response with results, we create attention getting ads that say absolutely nothing," he says.

The problem is people are so enthralled by the visuals that few recall the product or even the sponsor. Remember the puppy sock puppets of Super Bowl XXXIV? What company sponsored them? Are they still in business?

Forbes Magazine reported that Internet companies paid an average of $2.2 million for 30-second spots in that game, amounting to more than $40 million dollars. It was called the dot-com bubble's Waterloo. On the other hand, GoDaddy.com doubled its market share with a go-for-broke Super Bowl ad several years ago, so while it's a big gamble, it's not always a losing proposition.

GoDaddy continues on a roll. During the 2009 Superbowl, GoDaddy earned millions of hits based on the clever tactic of using its ad to drive Internet users to see "what they couldn't show on TV." Curious clickers saw spokesperson Danica Patrick take a shower as directed by teenage boys. Of course, the spoof showed nothing but PG rated fun as Danica turned the tables on them while pitching viewers to sign up. Now that's multi-level marketing!

Of course, small businesses don't have a multi-million dollar ad budget. But let not your heart be troubled. Advertising sales are very competitive, especially on local cable systems, and your local media outlets have salespeople who are very sophisticated.

The good news is you've got a friend in the business! Reps know if your ads don't pull in business it's unlikely you'll be back. They have a great deal of demographic information available, but you've got to talk with your sales rep to interpret it. They know their paper's readership numbers and, in the case of electronic media, will know when their audiences tune in by age, income, and preferences. But their time spent in providing this information will depend on your own interest. In other words, set uninterrupted time aside when you meet with them.

One caveat. Use due diligence. Utilize the ad rep's expertise and information to the greatest extent possible. However, understand s/he is selling for a single outlet and won't volunteer information on their competitors. It's up to you to contact media outlets in your advertising area and gather their information for your own assessment.

There's also a wealth of information on the Internet. One of them available at the time of this writing is www.zipskinny.com. Just type in a zipcode and it will list information on educational levels, income, marital status, racial breakdown, gender, occupation, and even percentages of home ownership in the area.

Knowing this information is valuable because it can help you shape your advertising to audience segments. The information is based on the US census so it will be dated since it's only updated every 10 years. Your local TV or radio ad rep will have more current data.

Yes, this takes time. But considering the cost of advertising, this is an instance where time truly is money. You'll also learn a lot about area demographics and trends, which will benefit you in the long run.

Innovative entrepreneurs see trends developing and prepare for them. Businesses that reach out to community groups to build trust will have a leg up on competitors who don't. Plan for the future because change is the only constant in life. This also applies to new or growing community groups. Se hable?

Getting the media to write a story on your business

"It's good to keep in mind that prominence is always a mix of hard work, eloquence in your practice, good timing and fortuitous social relations."

Barbara Kruger, artist, graphic designer

Actually, most newspapers will carry a short blurb about a new business but you need to know how to best present the facts to the reporter. Even better, know which reporter to contact. Have your one-minute commercial ready to go and don't ramble on.

Every paper has a business reporter. If you don't know who that is, call the news desk and ask. Read the paper to see how business news is presented and emulate that style and language. Most reporters prefer e-mail because the information only needs to be edited rather than rekeyed into their computers.

That said, <u>understand there is absolutely no requirement for any newspaper, radio or TV station to carry your information</u>. Therefore, be grateful for any free blurb you get, even if it's two lines out of the two pages you sent.

Although the media tout the ethical separation of the advertising and news departments, some small town editors will suggest if you buy advertising, you will be more likely to have an accompanying story done about your business.

Unless you have no need to ever have a relationship with the editor again, fight any urge to remind her that this sounds like she wants to be paid to run your story because it will be perceived as an ethical insult.

Put another way, it's folly to argue with people who buy ink by the barrel and paper by the ton, for they will always have the last word – even if that "word" is to ban you from the publication because you rubbed them the wrong way.

Similarly, reporters and editors are human and occasionally make mistakes. If you believe you've been misquoted or misrepresented, it's OK to make a polite call to the editor to make your feelings known. But keeping your cool can be the difference between an obscure correction on page 19 and a more prominent piece, or even a follow up story. (It can happen.) Even if you don't get satisfaction this time, remember you're in it for the long haul.

Additional thoughts

Think on multiple levels in getting your story out. This can be as simple as finding an angle that makes your business different from your competitors or from the many other types of enterprises out there.

Do you provide a unique service? Are your employees different from the norm, i.e., fully certified in what they do, younger than average, retired, involved in public service, award-winners, or stand out in some way?

<u>This is really important for non-profit organizations.</u> By their nature, non-profits are seen in a better light because of their community outreach function. Editors and news directors see covering these as a public service of their own and tend to provide greater coverage if given newsworthy material.

This built-in advantage can offset the smaller advertising budgets of many non-profits. Look for ways to regularly communicate about your organization's people, projects and accomplishments. Keeping your name in front of your publics increases recognition and credibility. That pays off in greater cash and material donations and more community engagement with your events. A check presentation is an opportunity for a photo with a short press release that reminds people about you while highlighting the donor.

For-profit businesses should use the same logic when they present gifts to community organizations. Have someone snap a photo as you present a check or other donation to the local Boys & Girls Club or food bank. You will bring attention to both organizations.

Many business owners have expertise in more than one area. Outside talents or involvements might make you interesting to interview even if your comments are not specifically related to your business. I knew the owner of a printing business who was a pilot and aviation history buff. He was not only interviewed on aviation matters but also published a pictorial book about vintage aircraft.

Community service and good will are quantifiable assets of any business. In fact, much of the valuation of a business has to do with good will. An accountant friend runs a fundraiser every Thanksgiving and Christmas to buy turkeys for homeless shelters. Local supermarkets anticipate his purchases and give him the best prices. While his work is motivated by concern for others, the good will he generates follows him.

We are creatures who operate in multiple spheres of influence. Folks who wear more than one hat in their community should use this to their advantage by talking about it. Until people get to know you, they really aren't interested in what you're doing. They want to know what you're going to do for them.

Good will is a key component of success. People do business with people they trust and like. Like "the better bones and healthy bodies" built by Wonder Bread of a past generation, good will builds public approval that increases visibility and helps to offset negative perceptions when things occasionally go wrong.

That having been said, press materials on a new or revamped business should have a definite focus. Don't swamp the reporter with irrelevant and confusing details that may have little to do with your basic message.

A new client once gave me more material about his past activities than his new enterprise. It was an example of content over context. Was he pitching a story about his past personal accomplishments or his new business? Put another way, the better prepared and focused your information is, the less time an editor or reporter needs to sift through the relevant facts and the more likely it is your story will be included.

A humorous story on spin – courtesy of the Internet – so you know it's true!

A genealogical researcher discovered a politician's great-great uncle was hanged for horse stealing and train robbery in Montana in 1889.

The only known photograph shows him standing on the gallows. On the back of the picture was an inscription identifying him as a horse thief sent to Montana Territorial Prison 1885, escaped 1887, robbed the Montana Flyer six times before being caught by Pinkerton detectives, convicted and hanged in 1889. He e-mailed the politician's staff for comments and received the revised biographical sketch:

"A famous cowboy in the Montana Territory, his business empire grew to include acquisition of valuable equestrian assets and intimate dealings with the Montana railroad. Beginning in 1883, he devoted several years of his life to service at a government facility, finally taking leave to resume his dealings with the railroad. In 1887, he was a key player in a vital investigation run by the renowned Pinkerton Detective Agency. In 1889, he passed away during an important civic function held in his honor when the platform upon which he was standing collapsed."

Branding

"Five exclamation marks, the sure sign of an insane mind."

Terry Pratchett, science fiction author

Branding, as the name implies, identifies a product or service with a person, business, or company. Branding is the exclamation point of a business.

Branding provides consistency in ads. Can you imagine MetLife without Snoopy, Budweiser without Clydesdales, or Disneyland without Mickey Mouse?

Branding associates products with identifiable images in the public eye. "Kleenex," "Xerox," and "Vaseline" became generic terms even though they represented specific products.

And what would KFC be without Colonel Sanders? Martha Stewart is her own brand. Branding campaigns can be national, regional, or even local, based on advertising and word of mouth, but they are established through consistency of message over time.

Though generally associated with big business, branding also applies to the small entrepreneur who develops a reputation or image of his or her own.

Branding becomes part of your corporate identity and an intangible part of your business. It is a connection that relies on consistency over time to establish and is worth hiring a graphic artist to bring to reality. Getting it right from the start is worth the investment. Your logo should be incorporated into every aspect of your business, including your letterhead, vehicles, website, advertising, mailers, signage, and business cards.

Coupled with paid advertising, <u>it can become the power of the relentless message</u>.

Mass customization

"Society does not consist of individuals but expresses the sum of interrelations, the relations within which these individuals stand."

Karl Marx, social scientist, revolutionary

That quote could just as easily be attributed to Edward L. Bernays, the aforementioned father of public relations. But while entrepreneurs today certainly believe in the concept of influencing the masses with key words, phrases and images, they are also personalizing their message.

During the past decade the term "mass customization" has become a business buzzword. It's a way to invite customer input into the creation of products and services, even down to the individual level. Here's how it's defined by Dr. Frank Piller, a faculty member of the MIT Smart Customization Group at the Massachusetts Institute of Technology:

> ***Meeting the needs of each individual customer:*** From a strategic management perspective, mass customization is a differentiation strategy. Customers gain from customization the increment of utility of a good that better fits to their needs than the best standard product attainable. The larger the heterogeneity of all customers' preferences, the larger is this gain in utility. From a managerial point of view, customization can be carried out with regard to *fit, style, and functionality*. To match the level of customization offered by a manufacturer with the customers' needs becomes a major success factor.

Home-based businesses communicate almost solely through the least expensive and most credible advertising of all, one-on-one personal contact. My favorite is **Market America**, which combines the personal approach of mass customization.

Founded in 1992, the company and has been growing exponentially in domestic and foreign markets. In addition to customized health products (a very big growth area), the company markets home, auto and pet care products in addition to providing links to hundreds of stores. As a communication specialist who saw this ever-growing company making all the right moves, I couldn't resist signing up.

My web portal is www.marketamerica.com/davidvincent. My e-mail there is dskocik@aol.com for additional information on this innovative, entrepreneurial company. (I'm using this vehicle to market to you – did you catch it?) Actually, I use and very much believe in these products, as do millions of my baby-boomer peers.

The same principle applies to business. Your office should serve as a customization of your business to customers. Keep product and service information readily available. Frame print stories and testimonial letters and hang them up or create a tasteful display for customers and prospects to see.

Create alliances with friends and acquaintances who belong to other organizations. Ask them to take you to their club or group and introduce you and your business. Many groups look for guest speakers or for tips for their monthly newsletters. Let others know you are available to share your expertise and insight.

Word of mouth advertising and testimonials

"Words are but symbols for the relations of things to one another and to us; nowhere do they touch upon absolute truth."

Friedrich Nietzsche, philosopher

As described by www.womma.org, the website of the Word of Mouth Marketing Association, Word of Mouth is the official trade association for the word of mouth marketing industry. Its mission is to promote and improve word of mouth marketing by:

- Promoting "best practices" to ensure more effective marketing
- Protecting consumers and the industry with strong ethical guidelines
- Evangelizing word of mouth as an effective marketing tool
- Setting standards to encourage its use

As previously noted, interpersonal contact is the most credible form of communication. Word of mouth, also known as "buzz marketing" and relationship marketing, can be powerful. If a family member or close friend tells you how effectively a product or service worked for them, it will likely carry a lot of weight in your own selection.

Everyone we come in contact with provides an opportunity to get the word out about what we do, including social clubs; public events; professional societies; friends; relatives; acquaintances; co-workers; places of worship, etc. Many home-based businesses like Amway and Mary Kay depend almost exclusive on word of mouth.

Get people talking about what you do. Encourage your customers to pass the word around. Tell them to let others know that if they mention who referred them, they will get a discount on their first visit. That implies, of course, that you will also provide a similar sweetener to the recommender.

Remember though, that this is only a step in the process. Don't rely solely on word of mouth because it depends on a relatively limited number of referrals. Early in our marriage, my wife and I shopped at a local store that had good quality furniture. The owner touted his prices made cheaper by his sole reliance on word of mouth advertising. We were loyal customers who told many people about him.

His business folded when competitors did an intense, months-long advertising campaign that steered prospects to their stores. Customers are fickle and must be communicated with repeatedly and on more than one level to maintain their loyalty and attention.

People do business with people they know and trust. For word-of-mouth marketing to work, you must build a strong relationship with your customers and proactively ask them to refer others to you.

The same applies to professional colleagues you refer people to, perhaps as the result of a leads exchange club. A key aspect of referring people to other professionals is that you are betting your own reputation they are trustworthy. That means getting together with them outside of networking meetings. They expect the same trustworthiness from you.

Customer testimonials never go out of style. Like word of mouth advertising, the personal referral is one of the strongest affirmations. When clients write a note praising your service, ask them if you may display their comments in your store or shop and offer to take a photo to include with it.

If they call record their contact information for possible follow up in an ad for your business. Note: Though most people will jump at the chance to be in an ad, <u>always</u> ask permission before using someone's name or photo. Better yet, get it in writing on a release form.

If the subject is a minor, get the parent to sign the release. Imagine the expense and trouble of having to reshoot a TV or print ad because one person in a large group decides he or she no longer wishes to be seen.

Additionally, the release should be time specific, i.e., "I authorize the use of my image and name in Johnson's Plumbing advertising campaign between April 1, and August 19, 20__."

Understand, because someone has signed the release or accepted a nominal sum of money doesn't necessarily mean they can't back out during the campaign. Though rare, if it happens honor the person's request and redo the ad. As always, if there's a concern, consult with your attorney before you spend time and money creating the ad.

When the ad comes out send a copy to the people depicted in it, whether print or electronic, along with a brief thank you note. For the electronic media, it's much easier if you let the TV or radio production team know ahead of time that you'll need copies later.

Providing expert advice

"I am amazed at how eager the CEOs of the biggest companies are today to communicate as effectively as possible, to employ the skills and the language ... They want to know that they can talk to a shareholder one-on-one, not just through their head but also through their heart. They want to know that they can reach their consumer not just on an intellectual basis, but on an emotional basis."

Frank Luntz, media consultant, in a 2004 interview with PBS Frontline.

Journalists are assigned to write stories on innumerable subjects. As such, their knowledge is a mile wide but often an inch deep on many subjects. When an international or national story breaks, editors look for a local angle.

Whether energy conservation, weight control, global warming, crime prevention, education, child care, or natural resources, editors or reporters focusing on localizing a story might call you for expert opinions if they know you're willing to offer them.

So how can you get the call, what with all your competitors out there? Here's the "secret." Reporters don't go to the yellow pages for sources. They call people who have contacted them or who have voiced opinions previously.

If what you do might have some interest to the public, pick up the phone and introduce yourself to reporters who focus on your area of expertise. Offer to be included in their contact list in the event they ever need information.

Provide a number where you can be reached immediately and follow up with an occasional e-mail reminder, but be judicious. Don't make reporters feel they are being stalked.

Speaking before groups

Author, speaker and Internet guru Tom Antion has given thousands of presentations on public speaking and is worth tracking down on the Internet at www.antion.com. Some of his top suggestions are below, but I recommend going to his website to purchase his video.

- Research the issues affecting your audience before you arrive so you sound like an insider.

- If you are planning to market yourself or your products in another country or language, make sure you understand the cultural system and the language. (Note: The same applies if you are marketing your services or goods to a new constituency in your local area. Be aware of cultural differences in specific groups.)

- Gauge the audience ahead of time for distribution of men and women. Women are less reserved and generally friendlier than men. They will laugh more readily at appropriate humor and are more receptive to head nodding agreement with the presenter, increasing their comfort level and the speaker's. Men tend to look to other men for agreement before they commit to enjoying themselves and will take longer to warm up.

- Early morning audiences will take longer to wake up and warm up

- Be enthusiastic. The audience will never be more motivated than the speaker.

- Involve members of the audience in the discussion to keep their attention.

The interview

"I will say that since our capture we have met with uniform kindness, and while in the penitentiary our relations with the officers have been cordially pleasant, and for their considerate and kind disposition we feel profoundly grateful."

Cole Younger, bank robber and killer, speaking for himself and brothers Jim and Bob, all serving life sentences at Stillwater, Minn., to author J.W. Buel, Nov. 7, 1880.

If ever there were an example of pure eloquence and kindness toward others from an unexpected source, that was it.

The News Story vs. The Feature Piece

There are two basic types of interviews, the news story and the feature piece. Treat them both seriously. Obviously, the news story will be about the basic facts that need to be communicated to the reader, usually on deadline. Be certain of your facts. It is better to say you'll get back to an interviewer than to shoot from the hip or speculate.

The feature story will be in depth, and generally not on tight deadline. These stories generally revolve around an individual of interest to the public, whether for positive or negative reasons. As such, the reporter may contact the subject several times with follow up questions. Always treat these contacts seriously.

As former head of public relations for a private college, I introduced the media to the expertise of our faculty through a monthly expert's list. Some faculty members were initially uncomfortable when approached about doing an interview. They feared being asked about something they couldn't answer. The same trepidation may affect you and the people who work for you.

I reassured them that people who practice a trade or perform a professional service for a living are indeed experts, and certainly have more knowledge and experience than the public at large and the reporter who will be doing the interview. It's the reporter's job to tell the story based on information that's already been determined to be important for readers to know.

Despite earlier concerns, the only post-interview question from faculty members was when they could do it again. If you've got a business that provides ongoing opportunities for media contacts and cultivation, by all means take advantage of it.

Some radio and TV reporters will ask for suggested questions or be receptive to them because this makes them seem more knowledgeable when the tape rolls. Offer to send, e-mail, or drop off background information for the reporter prior to your interview. Murphy's Law Note: Always have something in mind to talk about. I was once asked in a late afternoon call to substitute for my boss in a live TV interview early the next morning.

The subject was to be an update on the college I worked at but the exact purpose was unclear. I was told not to worry, just show up at the station and bring a list of questions for the reporter to ask. It was only when I arrived at the station was I told it was going to be a remote interview with the host of the show at the main studio 55 miles away. And even though I faxed the talking points to her before the interview, she never got the information.

Because she had no idea what to ask, she began by asking me to tell her what was going on at the college. (This was a definite sign that she had no clue who I was or what to ask.) I did a two-minute verbal tap dance, pausing every 20 seconds or so, hoping she'd jump in and save me, to no avail. In between pauses, I covered new academic programs, athletic successes, and upcoming campus events, hoping she'd pick up on one or more of those areas. No such luck.

Her follow up was to ask, "so what else is going on." Aaaarrrggghhh! Mercifully, her co-host took over, thanked me for talking to them and wrapped up the interview. Fear not. Though such an unplanned interview was probably a once-in-a-lifetime experience, having talking points ready to call up on a second's notice kept me from looking like a complete fool.

Some businesses have a formal press kit but often a brief information sheet will suffice. Feel free to include a quote or two, but be sure to include the source. This gives the reporter easy additional information to supplement the actual interview. Some press kits include background stories on the business or franchise. That's fine for establishing the company's history or credibility but don't swamp a reporter with company information if s/he has indicated the story is to be focused on you.

Although e-mail has become a part of both our business and personal lives, some folks still haven't learned it liabilities. Whether over the phone, in person, via e-mail or any other form of communication, ALWAYS assume whatever you say may be seen in print, including off-the-cuff remarks. Remember that e-mail is forever and has been successfully used in court cases. (Been there and done that.) Don't forward any e-mail you wouldn't want your mother to see in the local newspaper with your name under it.

Regardless of how familiar you may be with a reporter, always treat an interview or a press conference as a business event. A reporter's job is to convey information to the public in the most interesting manner possible and most do it very well. That may or may not include information you want published.

Even if a reporter agrees to go off the record (asking you to disclose sensitive background information to put the story in context but promises not to attribute it to you) are you willing to bet the ranch none of it will bleed into the published story? And what if you forget whether you're on the record or not? Nor are reporters required to honor requests to go off the record, particularly after you've already said something you regret. I recommend not going down that path.

We are living through a period of enhanced political correctness. Refrain from impromptu comments, particularly if they might offend someone if taken out of context. An "ice-breaking" joke about a person or group of people might end up being the focus of a story about corporate insensitivity. This also applies to comments before internal insider groups. More than one corporate executive has been embarrassed or unseated because of questionable comments recorded by unobtrusive mobile phone cameras that were later posted on the Internet.

Be comfortable with reporters. But remember that copy space is limited and side conversations on things having nothing to do with what you wish reported should be kept to a minimum because they might end up taking valuable space away from your story if mentioned.

Along those lines, when doing a radio or television interview, always assume the mike is on and what you say will be transmitted over the air. Many influential people, including several US presidents, have discovered this the hard way.

The press conference

"Publicity is a great purifier because it sets in action the forces of public opinion, and in this country public opinion controls the courses of the nation."

Charles Evans Hughes, 1862-1948, Chief Justice, US Supreme Court

Press conferences are called to unveil products and services, to discuss significant accomplishments or events, or to provide information during a crisis.

Except in the event of a crisis or emergency, they should be preceded by media notification at least three days prior to the event. The notification, which can be e-mailed, faxed, or called in, should include a brief reason for the press conference along with the day, date, time and location. Like a press release, it must include a contact person and phone number.

However, the notification should not contain all of the details of a press release, otherwise media representatives will have no reason to attend. Keep a record of everyone you called to prevent multiple calls or an overlooked name. Reporters are competitive and it doesn't pay to give one a scoop or ignore someone.

Have a press release ready to hand out at the press conference along with a media kit containing information on your business or product and background information on you. Make sure all of your handout material has a date on it. This helps prevent someone using old information for a story.

After the press conference, fax or e-mail your release to media that didn't make it to the event. Most who didn't show up will carry a brief notice about it. Never take the attitude that if-they-didn't-show-they-shouldn't-know. You will be the only one hurt by that. On broader events that include regional or national media, make sure you pay due diligence to the needs of your local press. They are the folks you live with.

Make notes while things are fresh in your memory. It will provide a great template for your next event as well as information for any follow up responses.

<u>It never hurts to have a colleague videotape or record your press conference</u>. It will prove valuable as a fact checker for what you actually said, a review of your technique and delivery style, as well as a record of who was there and what was asked in your debrief session.

What's a debrief session you ask? As previously stated, public relations is an ongoing process rather than an event. Debriefing is simply going over what was asked and how you responded.

- Could your answers have been more precise?
- Did you look professional?
- Were you able to bring up points relevant to the purpose of the event?

- Did you spend too much time on any one subject?
- Were you thrown off track by an unexpected question?
- Did you miss any key points?
- Did you have sufficient materials and resources?

The debriefing, particularly during a crisis, should be completed as soon as possible after the press conference while your memory and those of your team are fresh. That is when you will have the greatest support in requesting additional human and material resources if needed.

No shows

It's not necessarily a complete loss if the media doesn't come to a press conference or other event. Nor does it mean no one cares about what you have to say. I was once tasked with setting up an outdoor press conference to introduce a new service. Despite assurances from my media contacts that they would be there no one showed up. The client wasn't happy as we sweated in the muggy July sun.

Follow up calls to several editors revealed that the main water pump had broken down at the State Fair and everyone had been dispatched to an impromptu press conference the governor called to reassure visitors repairs were under way.

My client assumed all of our preparation was for naught. I proved my worth by calling editors to let them know that even though they had missed a great press conference on a relevant local story, I'd be happy to fax them the press release, along with doing a phone interview.

Since the only information they had was my version of reality, the release was carried in full, likely providing better coverage than if they had been there. Please note, I didn't lie; we held the press conference even though it was for our internal audience. Nor am I suggesting you ever try to deceive a reporter or editor. It will sooner or later come back to bite you.

The point is don't assume everybody hates you if there's little or no response. As previously noted, PR is a process, not an event. That's why Rhett Butler's most important comment to Scarlet O'Hara wasn't about not giving a damn, but that "tomorrow is another day."

The Internet – Websites

"While a calculator on the ENIAC is equipped with 10,000 vacuum tubes and weighs 30 tons, computers of the future may have only 1,000 vacuum tubes and weigh only 1.5 tons."

Popular Mechanics, 1949

"The newest computer can merely compound, at speed, the oldest problem in the relations between human beings, and in the end the communicator will be confronted with the old problem, of what to say and how to say it."

Edward R. Murrow, renowned journalist and commentator

Regarding the first prediction, imagine having to own a heavy-duty pickup truck to carry your personal computer around! It's clear the author never envisioned the portable laptop computer nor the technology that would make it possible.

Particularly interesting in the second quote is that Murrow died in 1965, nearly 30 years before the computer became a daily conduit of communication. Considering the computer is a flat medium that doesn't convey emotion but is used almost exclusively by many communicators today, Murrow's observation is truer than ever.

While traditional marketing channels include print and electronic, direct mail, billboard and directory advertising, new and emerging marketing opportunities include electronic distribution channels, website optimization, behavioral marketing, interactive relationships, consumer generated media, viral marketing, broadband and rich media mobile technology, and convergence technologies.

On a worldwide basis, in August 2008, the Radicati Group, a California-based company that covers email security, archiving, regulatory compliance, wireless technologies, web services, and identity management, conducted a study showing that the worldwide base of active mailboxes will increase from 2 billion in 2008 to over 2.7 billion in 2012. Each of these will send more than 200 messages daily. The numbers are mind boggling. See www.radicati. com

This subject has lent itself to entire books so I'll resist going into depth, particularly since this guide is focused on basic principles. Today's businesses have opportunities that increase monthly. Websites have become very inexpensive and can be purchased through vendors selling prepackaged sites needing only minor customization.

The web has become an increasingly relevant method of passing information along and despite the opportunity for mischief, is increasingly challenging traditional news and marketing channels for credibility. As former CBS newsman Dan Rather discovered in the 2004 election cycle, bloggers will challenge what they perceive to be questionable evidence of wrongdoing.

Websites and blogs have become the norm for businesses. Newspapers and TV stations are well aware of this and are creating increasingly sophisticated sites to capture the attention of growing numbers of people, particularly 18-to-34-year-olds, who rely on the web for their news and information.

National newspapers like the Wall Street Journal, the New York Times and USA Today all feature video presentations of the news. Like the NY Times, the newspapers work to show their sites are not just a reproduction of the print edition, but provide additional and exclusive content including articles, blogs, and videos.

But then so do some local dailies and weeklies, which even accept breaking video from cell phones contributors. I called a weekly hometown paper to offer photos of a fire in a client's business that had happened only hours earlier. The editor told me they already had video from a reporter's cell phone on their website.

In October 2008, the century-old Christian Science Monitor said it would discontinue its daily print edition in April 2009 and move almost exclusively to online publication, becoming the first major national newspaper to abandon a daily paper-and-ink format. The church-subsidized newspaper, which focuses on analysis of the news, is doing so for economic reasons.

The move is expected to save millions of dollars annually in printing costs and postage since the majority of its 50,000 geographically dispersed subscribers receive their paper by mail. Going electronic will also allow readers to see the paper the same day. However, to maintain its print presence the Monitor plans to publish a weekly magazine.

Like radio, the Internet is nearly instantaneous. AOL had photos of the January 10, 2009, NFL playoff game between the Arizona Cardinals and the Carolina Panthers online while the game was still in progress.

When it comes to web use and blogging, there really are "influencers," and they really do matter, according to a report by Rubicon Consulting. In a white paper published in October 2008, a broad survey of US web users confirmed that a small group of people dubbed MFCs "most frequent contributors" drive purchases by others.

Although they represent less than 10 percent of web users, MFCs are responsible for about 80 percent of user generated content on the web, including comments and questions about a service or product. The key finding is that their reviews are more influential on purchasing decisioning than official or manufacturer reviews. See www.rubiconconsulting.com for additional information.

Another user of the web and its social networking potential are political campaigns who employ specialists to engage bloggers and others who can help. They've capitalized on the Internet to seek volunteers, voter feedback, and donors. Their blogs allow them to sample and even shape public opinion on issues.

Similarly, nationwide businesses like NASCAR are capitalizing on the opportunities provided by the Internet. Their social networking focuses on the track experience and connects fans from across the country to encourage them to visit their tracks and participate in events that may be unique to each track.

In addition to racing, activities include camping, entertainment, track and local facilities, and the opportunity to develop relationships with other fans as the NASCAR brand is reinforced and buyer behavior is influenced. But most importantly, the goal will be to institute a dialog with fans to find out what they're thinking and what they want.

These and other efforts by businesses will be particularly important to maintain client bases affected by competition and economic recession.

In effect, if your business lends itself to social networking you've got to seriously engage prospects and consumers and figure out ways to show people you care about their needs and are listening to what they have to say. Contacts have got to be meaningful and more than just numbers contacted. Benchmarking is good, but return on investment is the bottom line here.

Most small businesses don't have the time or resources to fully jump into the social networking realm of blogging but they should be aware that it exists and is growing. It requires initiating and maintaining ongoing dialogue with others and actively seeking out and engaging opinion leaders. It won't overtake the importance of traditional media anytime in the near future but it is yet another level of contact for younger customers or prospects.

If you have a website, include the address on your letterhead, press releases, advertising, and on your signage.

Encourage people to comment on your service or product and post testimonials on your blog. Like YouTube, blogs can spread your message to interested parties across the country and beyond.

Some small businesses have gone global through dedicated sites of their own and commercial sites like eBay. The beauty of the Internet is there are no bricks and mortar, no overhead, and unlimited reach. The downside, of course, is there's also a lot of junk out there.

Type a keyword in your browser that relates to your business and look at examples of what competitors are doing, then try to differentiate yourself. If you decide to create a website, make certain it is regularly updated and provides an opportunity for feedback.

Tip: If your site contains institutional information about your company, make sure to include it as a boilerplate (standard) paragraph at the bottom of your releases, e.g., "Mack's Farm and Tractor Supply is a third-generation, award-winning, family-owned business that has supported the Hometown Boys and Girls Club for 50 years."

Not only will editors sometimes include boilerplate information like this; they have also been known on a slow news day to assign a reporter to write a story on it. (Where do you think Charles Kuralt and Charles Osgood got their ideas?)

Conversely, make certain to include links to previous publicity on your website, such as stories and even press releases about your business. This redundancy provides visitors additional opportunities to learn about you. Use the most current and relevant material to keep visitors coming back. Use good judgment in the amount of information you include. Visitors, like newspapers readers, will bypass cluttered pages.

Note: Be sure there are links on each of your webpages that lead back to your homepage, otherwise the visitor will just continue surfing to other websites, probably to your competitors.

Have someone review your site periodically to make certain it's current, interesting, and not overly complicated. Some companies require their sites to be updated every six months. The purpose of the site is to attract and inform visitors, not to overload their senses.

Web technology has become increasingly sophisticated with photos, streaming video, talking heads, and even product demonstrations. Search engines will often pick up local news articles by category and even letters to the editor if your local paper publishes to the web. In other words, an essay you pen about ways to improve efficiency in someone's business or home may put your name in lights far beyond the local area, so include your e-mail address for follow up comments and contacts. The same applies when you write an article or a letter to the editor.

YouTube has gained a great deal of popularity with its short videos submitted by everyday people. I'm not suggesting you upload an informational video on YouTube, although some have done this successfully. The problem is once it's online, you lose control over its distribution and it may stay there forever.

The point is that a growing number of people are spending more time online and online commerce is increasing exponentially every year. It might be to your advantage to set up a web merchant account.

E-mail lists

In establishing a personal relationship built on trust and credibility, a growing number of businesses use e-mail to contact their customers and prospects. Some chambers of commerce, not wanting to miss out on a profit center, are providing E-Blast, where for a fee they will e-mail your advertisement to all of their members.

It is estimated that as many as 90 percent of messages are unsolicited spam. If you decide to communicate with your customers or prospects via unsolicited e-mail, be wary of too-frequent contact and give people the opportunity to opt out, lest you unwittingly become a spammer who's blocked by your provider from sending e-mails.

Include a request for e-mail addresses on your next customer survey sheet and explain they have the option of receiving everything you send out or just specific categories of information, e.g., sales, new products, consumer tips, or online greeting cards. Then it's up to you to create e-mail groups. Consider setting up a quarterly e-letter that provides useful information and encourages feedback. Make sure you indicate you will never share or sell your list.

Let people know they can also contact you via e-mail if they have a question. It's better to provide a business e-mail address rather than a personal one. It looks more professional, has a better chance of not being screened out by spam filters looking for common URLs, and will keep your business and personal correspondence separate.

If you have a webpage ask your provider if they offer statistics so you know who is visiting your site, whether it's from a direct link, a search engine, or through a link from another site. Contact other businesses who might be willing to partner with you by exchanging web links.

You can build up your address list by getting people to respond to your website and capturing their email addresses. As long as you're giving them something they can use – expert tips, humor, or some other information that makes your notes worthwhile to read -- they will be open to your sales pitch because they know and trust you.

Depending on the size of their business, some owners will pass their personal cell phone number along to top customers. That works with personal consultants, but will not likely work well with a high volume business. The key is to establish communication guidelines that are responsive to customers and clients, yet manageable to you and your staff.

In other words, it's ok not to engage in every communication option. Decide what's doable. You can't be all things to all people. Choose the areas of communication that are important to you and that you can do well. It's better not to promise email responses or forgo blogging if you don't have the staffing to do it right.

5

How do I do ...

The press release

"Publicity is the life of this culture - in so far as without publicity capitalism could not survive - and at the same time publicity is its dream."

John Berger, art critic, novelist, painter

A press release is merely a notice that something happened or is going to happen. It can announce a new business, product, service, or personal accomplishment.

A release should not contain redundant or repetitive information because it adds to the length, bores the reader, and discourages the editor from wanting to rewrite it.

Remember, unlike broadcast scripts, the print reader has the opportunity to go back and review information. And, of course, releases should be done on a word processor, rather than handwritten.

A press release, unlike creative writing, should always be:

- Joe Friday format – just the facts. Don't prattle on;
- Double-spaced (if mailed or faxed) and not more than two pages long;

- Written in Associated Press inverted pyramid style with as many of the "who, what, when, where and why" elements in the first sentence or two;

- Spellchecked;

- Reviewed for grammar and accuracy by another reader;

- Transmitted via e-mail so as not to have to be rekeyed by the receiver

The top of the release should contain the OK to release the information immediately -- as noted in the following sample release -- or the words EMBARGO UNTIL when you want a delayed publication, the date, the contact person, and the contact phone number. Following is an example, but there are multiple styles.

FOR IMMEDIATE RELEASE   June 12, 20__
CONTACT: Mike Smith   (123) 456-7890

Free Internet Seminar

HOMETOWN: *Mike's Internet Publishing and Web Service* will host a free seminar on "How to use the Internet to Sell Products," on Monday, July 1, from 7 to 9 p.m., at its offices on 123 Elm Street, Hometown, NJ.

Owned by and operated by Mike and Darlene Smith, the specialty business opened its doors in 2008 in response to the need of small, home based businesses to get the most from Internet business site providers.

"Business has been great but we get calls from people wanting to know more about what we do, so Darlene and I decided to host this free event to help others maximize their potential," said Mr. Smith.

Call (123) 456-7890 by June 27 to register.

(Blah, blah, blah, including your mission statement and website, but not more than two pages total, if possible.)

###

Note: The pound mark means the end. In a printed release use – MORE - centered at the bottom of the page if there are following pages, and use the slug below on the following page followed by the page number on the upper left corner of the following page(s). This is done in case the pages of a printed release get separated.

MIKE'S INTERNET PUBLISHING
2-2-2-2

However, <u>if you send your release via e-mail, disregard this note</u>, since multiple pages are all in the same document and not differentiated by pagination.

Style, format and proofreading

Journalists write in Associated Press (AP) style and if you mimic that standard you will increase your chances of being published. AP style, which is different than creative writing used for feature stories and novels, uses the inverted pyramid where the most important facts come first.

Those are the five Ws – who, what, where, where, why (and how). I teach my journalism students to try to include as many of these elements in the first paragraph as possible, and that the first paragraph should ideally be only one sentence. Look at your local newspaper to prove this. Whatever you do, however, make it interesting and understandable. That means you will end up writing and rewriting your release multiple times.

The added benefit of putting the important information up top is that if an editor decides to include your release but only has a small space to fill, s/he knows the first couple sentences can be used without having to rewrite the story. Publication success is often a matter of time and timing. An editor on a short timeline will use a well-written story over one that needs work on clarity and grammar.

Assume the reader knows nothing about you or your business. Avoid acronyms, but they may be used after the first reference is spelled out. Remember you're an expert in your field and an abbreviation or term that seems commonplace or logical to you may have no meaning to another person.

Think of a press release as a business letter. It should be to the point and contain all the pertinent facts but not a lot of unnecessary information – it's the grade A hamburger, not the hamburger helper. The practice of using double, or 1 ½ line spacing on releases is based on the dated premise of leaving room to allow for editing marks. It also serves to make the text look more readable. Of course, nearly all press releases are sent electronically today and the editor can manipulate the text without having to rekey it.

Avoid writing large blocks of text. Look at how newspapers are laid out. The first sentence, or "lead," is generally the first paragraph. Paragraphs in print are rarely more than two or three sentences. That's done to draw the reader in and keep him reading the entire story. Large blocks of text discourage the reader.

Avoid redundancies that make the release longer and harder to convert to a usable document. It is to your advantage to emulate AP style in releases because anything that makes the editor's and reporter's job easier increases your chances of appearing in print.

NOTE: Always, always (yes, I repeated "always" for emphasis) have someone proofread anything you send out, no matter how many times you've gone over it, for grammar, content and spelling. It's embarrassing to send something out only to realize the next day that it contains misspellings, poor grammar, incomplete sentences, or incorrect information.

This rule also applies to letters to the editor, which are often fired off in haste and without sufficient attention to grammar or editing for clarity. Editors don't always review submissions for libelous statements, nor do they assume responsibility for correcting grammatical or factual errors, often just pasting in what they receive.

Don't be a DIP

Incidentally, as I teach my communication students, the three elements of libel are easy to remember: **DIP** or Defamation, Identification, and Publication. Don't be a DIP and you won't end up on the wrong side of a libel suit. Defamation is publishing something that harms another's reputation; Identification is using a name or clear reference to another; Publication is printing or emailing it to a 3rd party. Reprinting or retransmitting it is another libel.

That doesn't mean you can avoid trouble if you simply say it (slander) rather than print it. You can libel someone on TV or radio as well. Although truth is the ultimate defense, court fights are expense and ugly.

The need for accuracy is especially true for websites. While a print document is often in front of readers for a short time, a website just sits there until someone changes it. This is another reason to regularly review and update your website.

Accuracy reflects directly on your professionalism, even if someone else wrote the release for you. A fall back, if no one is available to proof your material, is to print it and slowly read it aloud. Doing this forces you to see every word.

Virginia Tech offers a proofreading website that explains when we read normally, we often see only the shells of words -- the first and last few letters. We fix our eyes on the print only three or four times per line or less, and the average reader can only take in six letters accurately with one fixation.

It advises, "In proofreading, you can take nothing for granted, because unconscious mistakes are so easy to make. It helps to read out loud, because 1) you are forced to slow down and 2) you hear what you are reading as well as seeing it, so you are using two senses. It is often possible to hear a mistake, such as an omitted or repeated word that you have not seen."

Professional editors proofread as many as ten times. Publishing houses hire teams of readers to work in pairs and errors still occur. This is not true of newspapers, however, which will often paste in what they receive, errors and all.

The following is taken from an anonymous source on the Internet. It proves our minds are capable of overlooking major typos.

> Cna yuo raed tihs? i cdnuolt blveiee taht I cluod aulaclty uesdnatnrd waht I was rdanieg. The phaonmneal pweor of the hmuan mnid, aoccdrnig to a rscheearch at Cmabrigde Uinervtisy, it dseno't mtaetr in waht oerdr the ltteres in a wrod are, the olny iproamtnt tihng is taht the frsit and lsat ltteer be in the rghit pclae. The rset can be a taotl mses and you can sitll raed it whotuit a pboerlm. Tihs is bcuseae the huamn mnid deos not raed ervey lteter by istlef, but the wrod as a wlohe. Azanmig huh? yaeh and I awlyas tghuhot slpeling was ipmorantt!

Proofread the following paragraph. Review it once and write down the number of mistakes you catch. * Answers are in the next section.

In following the path we set for ourselves or that others set for us, it's is often very difficult to determine the the right course of actoin in a difficult situation. Too take the path of lest resistance will challenge you're conscience. We all want to be lead down the right path. Then again and ultimately, this makes the difference in who we are. Its a real dilemma but makes alot of difference.

Check and recheck

Avoid sending something out the same day you write it. It's amazing how a night's sleep can improve one's ability to notice ambiguities, redundancies, and grammatical errors, as well as to change perspective. What seems like a great idea one day may not the next.

A fellow PR practitioner asked an intern to write a release about a free seminar entitled "The Art of Public Relations." Unfortunately, neither he nor she noticed the omitted "l" in public. There must have been an interesting crowd at that event.

Include the day with the date of an event since readers think in those terms. Hint: keep a calendar next to your computer to verify that days always match dates.

Always use care in listing phone numbers where typos are likely to go unnoticed. An accomplished fund raising professional I once worked with organized a ladies tea social to cultivate prospects for a non-profit organization.

The content was checked by several people for grammar, spelling, date, location, and time. It was only after she began receiving calls from a local liquor store about elderly women responding to the invitation did she realize she had transposed the last two digits of the contact number. It was a classic example of Murphy's Law. Although she later laughed about it, she knew she lost more in respect from her audience than she did in wasted time, money, special paper and postage.

The lesson to be learned? Unless it's your own phone number, call any number listed on an invitation or press release to make certain it's the right number, especially if someone else passed it along to you.

Smith or Smyth? John or Jon?

Never misspell someone's name. It's an insult that shows you didn't care enough to check. Unless you know for certain, don't assume common spellings of names are accurate. Such mistakes are more common than most realize.

If necessary, call the person to verify spelling and middle initial. It's much less embarrassing than getting it wrong in print. Also, if you're going to include any biographical or professional information about someone, run it by him/her first. Misstating facts about someone could result in a lawsuit. The person will thank you for calling to check. The same applies to getting titles right, including academic and religious designations.

Be careful of contractions, particularly when using "it's" and "its." Unlike every other word, "its" is the possessive case. "It's" is <u>always</u> a contraction for "it is." If you're still confused, just say "it is" to yourself before you write "it's" to see if it fits.

Other common mistakes include plural possessives. Plural possessives are formed by adding only an apostrophe after the S or ES in the plural form, e.g., the girls' dresses. If the plural doesn't end in an S, add an apostrophe S, e.g., the children's classroom. If you're still confused, or the sentence doesn't flow well, recast the sentence.

A general note: as a professional businessperson try your best to speak as you write. If you wouldn't write "me and him," don't say it. Speak like the pillar of the community that you are. People will notice. Here again are several examples from the Virginia Tech website:

"Which of the following is correct?

- Two students -- John and *me* -- solved the problem.
- Two students -- John and *I* -- solved the problem.
- The problem was solved by two students, John and *me*.
- The problem was solved by two students, John and *I*.

Judging which is correct requires the definition of *appositive:* A noun or noun substitute set beside another noun or noun substitute and identifying or explaining it.

Example: I met Maria, a *physicist.* [*Physicist* is in apposition with *Maria.*]

Rule: An appositive takes the same case as the noun or pronoun with which it is in apposition. Thus, only the <u>second and third of the foregoing sentences are correct.</u>

* Check and recheck (Answers to previous section on proofreading)"

In following the path we set for ourselves or that others set for us, it's <u>is</u> often very difficult to determine the <u>the</u> right course of <u>actoin</u> in a difficult situation. <u>Too</u> (To) take the path of <u>lest</u> (least) resistance will challenge <u>you're</u> (your) conscience. We all want to be lead (led) down the right path. Then again and ultimately, this makes the difference in who we are. <u>Its</u> (It's) a real dilemma but makes alot (a lot) of difference.

Some commonly misspelled words include: A lot, accidentally, accommodate, all right, anoint, battalion, broccoli, cemetery, consensus, coolly, definitely, despair, desperate, desiccate, development, dissipate, drunkenness, ecstasy, embarrassment, exceed, existence, harass, inadvertent, indispensable, inoculate, insistent, irresistible, irritable, judgment, liaison, liquefy, miniscule, memento, millennium, occasion, occurrence, privilege, pursue, receive, recommend, repetition, sacrilegious, seize, separate, supersede, subpoena, tyranny, yield, weird.

Photos

"The caterpillar does all the work but the butterfly gets all the publicity."

George Carlin, comedian

A picture is truly worth a thousand words if properly shot. In fact, a good picture can be worth more than the story it accompanies if it draws attention to the piece. Always think creatively and take multiple shots so you can select the best one.

If possible, include a photo with a press release. If you make a presentation to a local group, sign a sizable contract, or unveil a new product or service, set up a photo "grip and grin" event (two people shaking hands, facing the camera) and create a short release. Attach the photo to the release and e-mail it to your media contacts.

For those who don't own one, a digital camera with the equipment necessary to interface with your computer can cost as little as $50.

If you transmit a follow up press release after an event, include a digital photo. If for some reason your newspaper won't accept attachments (very rare today), the fallback is to paste a photo into the text of your electronic release.

Just because a reporter didn't show up doesn't mean your story won't be used as a filler on a slow day. Never assume you're wasting time sending a press release or snapping photos. <u>Caveat:</u> Resist the urge to send more than one or two photographs or any graphics that will take more than a few seconds to download.

Think about composition. Photos should convey action and emotion.

Will an editor prefer a picture of you behind the counter of your pet store or a child happily bringing home a kitten or petting a puppy?

How about the choice between Santa Claus visiting your store or a child waiting in line to see him? Which one will more likely draw a reader's eye to your story?

Remember that the viewer's eye will naturally be drawn to images of people, children or animals over pictures of well-stocked shelves or equipment.

The Public Service Announcement (PSA)

Like a press release, the PSA conveys information and is run free of charge. It should be delivered 10 days to two weeks before the event to print media and about 30 days out for electronic media, especially TV, which has a longer lead time for their announcement pages.

Note, however, that a PSA is generally about a no cost or low-cost event to which the public is invited. It could be a free seminar on financial planning, a school play, a church bazaar, a fund raiser, or to raise public awareness about an issue. PSAs from for-profit businesses have little chance of being carried unless there's a clear public service component.

Though free, it is always carried at the discretion of the editor or news director. As with a press release, be thrifty in word usage and avoid redundancy. If you're writing a PSA for use on the radio, time it so it can be read in about 30 seconds.

The following sample is similar to what is routinely submitted to local radio stations: "The Ladies Community Volunteer Society, formed in 1987 by concerned women in the metropolitan area, will host a dinner fundraiser at the society's clubhouse on Main Street in Hometown. This will be a special event because it marks the 15th anniversary of the dinner. The society was founded to make the downtown a better area and to improve elementary education in center city. The dinner will raise funds for a new playground at the Ellimastric Public Daycare Center. The time is 7 p.m. on August 13. Tickets can be purchased or reservations made by calling 123-456-7891. The reservation deadline is August 7, and no tickets will be available at the door."

Here's how it might be rewritten for the announcer, minus the "hamburger helper," but with the phonetic spelling.

THE LADIES COMMUNITY VOLUNTEER SOCIETY IN HOMETOWN WILL HOST A DINNER FUNDRAISER ON

SATURDAY, AUGUST THIRTEENTH AT SEVEN P.M.. THE DINNER WILL BENEFIT A NEW PLAYGROUND AT THE ELLIMASTRIC (ELLA-MASS-TRICK) PUBLIC DAYCARE IN CENTER CITY. THE EVENT WILL ALSO CELEBRATE THE FIFTEENTH ANNIVERSARY OF THE SOCIETY. CALL 123-456-7890 FOR TICKETS. THE RESERVATION DEADLINE IS AUGUST SEVENTH. THAT'S 123-456-7890 FOR TICKETS.

The whole point is that the easier you make it for the media to process your information, the greater the chance it will be carried. Tweaking your information and reviewing it with others before you submit it will also cause you to focus on the important points as well as provide the opportunity for feedback and correction of errors or additional information you may have overlooked. As with a press release, make sure there's a contact number for follow up questions.

Deadlines

"A deadline is negative inspiration. Still, it's better than no inspiration at all."

Rita Mae Brown, mystery novelist

When you communicate with the media, always bear in mind their publication deadlines. When a reporter calls a source for information on breaking news, s/he often has a very short deadline and may be working on multiple stories. Waiting until you have more time to return the call tells the reporter you are unreliable as a timely source of information.

In getting routine information to the news desk for possible assignment to a reporter, plan for a timely release just as you plan for client jobs. Give daily newspapers at least a week's notice of an event you would like them to cover (which is longer than notification of a press conference.)

For last-minute press releases, the absolute deadline for daily newspapers is generally three days prior to publication; for weeklies, don't even think about getting information to them less than a week out. Even then, your late information will fall in the queue behind everyone else looking for free ink and you probably won't be published that week, if at all.

For feature stories in magazines, the deadline is often <u>two or three months</u> before the publication date. Therefore, if you've been thinking about pitching a seasonal story to a magazine, plan a whole season ahead.

<u>When in doubt, call</u>. Go online or to the phone book and compile a list of every newspaper, radio, and TV station in your area. Create a computer file that can be easily updated. Add additional info, such as deadlines, personal contact numbers, etc., as necessary.

Radio

Radio is considered a "hot" medium in that you can respond directly to it – except of course, during prerecorded programs. Radio has been called the "theater of the mind," because listeners create their own mental images of what the announcer describes.

Because production is simple compared to the visual requirements of television, advertisers can create spots in a very short period and very cheaply. Radio is more local and responsive to short-notice announcements, whether commercial or public service, like traffic reports or accident notification.

Radio is also ideal for on-air promotion. Some stations do paid remote broadcasts at businesses, inviting customers to come down to meet their air personalities. The entire broadcast becomes a commercial for the business, which often combines special sales or giveaways during the broadcast to attract customers, along with interviews of the business owner.

Though not generally a direct means of promoting one's business, don't discount calling talk shows if you hear a discussion concerning your area of expertise. It also doesn't hurt to pitch an idea for a show that includes you as the guest to the station manager or host. As hockey great Wayne Gretzky said, "you miss 100 percent of the shots you never take."

Remember, media is focused on providing service to their advertisers and listeners. Talk shows need guests every day. If you can provide information to help people do something, save money, improve their lives, or even entertain them, make the call.

If you're involved with a cutting-edge business where information changes or is regularly updated, there's nothing wrong with e-mailing or faxing radio or TV hosts about a hot topic. You may be called to do an interview. Touch bases quarterly to remind the media you're available to offer expert advice on a current topic.

Publicly expressing your knowledge in your professional realm is a giant step toward being seen as a recognized expert and the "go to" person. Don't worry about being grilled on all of the aspects of what you do. Radio hosts speak to their audiences in general terms and seek informed opinions. People will remember your name long after the particular subject you discussed. Hint: to help keep your train of thought while on the air, jot down the points you want to make (and the name of the host) while you're waiting your turn.

Note: Keep a file of your press clippings and letters to the editor that document your expertise. Keep an e-file you can send to the media to establish your credibility. Link it to your website. But again, don't overwhelm readers with information.

The TV Interview

"Regardless of how you feel inside, always try to look like a winner. Even if you are behind, a sustained look of control and confidence can give you a mental edge that results in victory."

Arthur Ashe, legendary tennis player

Virtually all cable TV stations having exclusive rights to serve communities must set aside time for local public interest programming. This is the reason for interview programs featuring local people and issues.

Although broadcast stations licensed under the Federal Communications Commission operate under different rules than cable stations, cable providers are also answerable to the public as well as the local government.

Watch local news programs and note the hosts' names, topics, and interview styles. Determine how your business may fit their format and contact them. Some stations have half-hour slots, others only five minutes. But then again, what would it cost you to buy five minutes of TV or radio time to promote your expertise? If you are fortunate enough to land a spot, treat it like the opportunity it is and come prepared.

Practice your presentation before family or friends, or even before a mirror. Watch your facial expressions. Get comfortable with yourself and enjoy the opportunity. Your goal is to establish yourself as the "resident expert" so that others will want to come to you for follow up engagements or interviews. It's not only good for the ego, but also for business.

TV hosts are regular people. When you meet them before the interview, look them in the eye, remember their names, give a firm handshake, and know something about them. You'll feel more comfortable, and so will they.

TV likes visual action. Don't jump up and down or wave your arms but be expressive when you speak. Watch how local announcers move their heads and hands when they deliver the news. Generate excitement about yourself and your product or service by showing honest enthusiasm.

During the interview, do your "commercial" without having to obviously resort to notes. But don't be a fast talker, trying to verbally download everything you know. Keep your answers to several sentences if possible. A good way to prep is to watch others being interviewed by the reporter or host who will be talking with you. Your pre-interview homework includes observing how others present themselves and judging what you consider to be their best points.

Time flies, especially on television, so as with a press release, give your most important information first. It's OK to give the host a brief list of suggested questions to cover ahead of time, with the most important up top. But don't assume they will all be asked because the interviewer may want to know about other things. Whatever the question, acknowledge it, give your response, the STOP to provide time for the next question.

Expect to have time to cover only the key points of the information you want to impart. That's why it's important to rehearse your answers with someone before the interview. If you have to think about what you're saying, you will look uncomfortable.

The best interviews are conversational, with you and the host interacting in a friendly give-and-take manner. After all, if you're not comfortable describing your product or service, you can't expect the public to want it. Since most interviews are pre-taped in a quiet studio you won't have an audience. Even if you do have an audience, focus on the interviewer as though you're having a private conversation and relax. Smile. Relax. Breathe. You'll come across better.

For multi person or panel interviews, body language expert Patti Wood says when people complete what they're saying, they may drop their arms and lean back close their mouth and make eye contact as a way to seek feedback on what they said and in effect allow someone else a turn to speak

Finally, for on-location interviews there are rare times when a reporter isn't available at your location and you may be asked to do a live remote interview with the camera person holding the mike as you speak with the anchor in the newsroom. This is when preparation meets opportunity!

You'll be given a headset or earpiece. Not a problem, just relax and look into the lens pretending there's a little person inside. It's really not much different than a phone conversation. And because the message is more visual than audio, remember to smile.

6

Special Circumstances –
Unexpected challenges & surprises

Backlash

"A reputation once broken may possibly be repaired, but the world will always keep their eyes on the spot where the crack was."

Joseph Hall, theologian of the Reformation

Backlash is an unintended consequence of an action. Good intentions may go awry through no fault of yours and negatively impact your project or personal credibility.

In November 2008, CEOs from the Big Three auto companies came to D.C. to ask Congress for bailout money. They cited the dire straits U.S. auto makers were in and the need for taxpayer money. When it was revealed they had flown in on corporate jets for the hearings, they lost sympathy with the press, the public at large, and most importantly, Congress. Even worse, several of them defended their perks as entitlements, showing they just didn't get it.

Weeks later, they returned in hybrid autos. Several promised not only to reject multi-million bonuses but to work for only $1 a year until their financial crisis was resolved, much as Lee Iacocca did decades earlier to save Chrysler. Ford's CEO also went on YouTube with a reassuring message that his company was working to make certain they would come out of this a better company.

In December 2008, a contractor for the U.S. Army sent 7,000 letters to the relatives of soldiers killed in Iraq and Afghanistan. The intent of the letter was to inform family members about private organizations offering assistance and support. Unfortunately, due to an oversight, the "Dear John Doe," salutation offended many sensibilities. The Army quickly followed up with sincere apologies, but the error made national news. How could anyone in the process not have noticed this clear mistake before the letters went out?

In 2006, a Los Angeles company advertised its bottled water as "not bottled in Cleveland." Perhaps the ad agency thought Cleveland would make an easy target or wouldn't find out about their ad. Bad assumption.

Cleveland officials ran comparison tests and announced that their tap water from Lake Erie had no arsenic while the company's bottled water contained 6.3 micrograms of arsenic per liter. The company responded their water only had 2 micrograms of arsenic per liter. It was one of those I-really-only-beat-my-dog-occasionally responses. While this tiff generated national publicity for its product, it was not the kind the company planned.

Unanticipated publicity can also be the result of a business blaming injuries from its product on users. Witness the lawsuits generated against a major tire company when it suggested product failures were the fault of poor driving practices and the auto manufacturer that was using its product.

The lesson to be learned from these examples is never forget the importance of perception and don't make comparisons with your competitors unless you're familiar with their products – and yours.

Another example might be a business that distributes toys to needy families at Christmas only to discover one of the toys has small pieces that have been swallowed by several children. While the company is not the manufacturer, the fact that its employees handed them out may result in some liability.

The company's response could be the difference between being forgiven or sued out of business. The best rule of thumb is to think logically and personally. How people react to a business that has injured a family member will likely depend a great deal on how the business responded to them.

If its first reaction were to blame the victim for not using the product properly or an outright denial of all responsibility, it's likely they will have to retain a good defense lawyer.

If, however, the CEO or her spokesperson were to immediately issue a statement of concern about anyone who might have been harmed, along with a request to call a hotline with concerns, the outcome might be different. She might also ask people to return the toys for a reward.

This assumes she consulted her attorney, who would likely have advised her to be careful not to accept responsibility while expressing concern. That's understandable. But the difference between the two approaches reflects someone concerned about her community vs. only caring about defending the business.

People often sue because they're angry at being ignored or treated poorly. One can win the legal battle and lose in the court of public opinion. Businesses must be proactive rather than reactive in events and issues that spill into the media because the public naturally tends to sympathize with the little guy who has seemingly been wronged.

The foregoing is a scenario that the average small business person likely won't encounter. Remember, however, that people will react to you the way they believe you perceive them. Deal honestly and forth righteously with others and they will give you the benefit of the doubt in questionable situations.

That being said, you will sleep better at night if you have a plan in place.

Crisis communication

"People don't really care how much you know until they know how much you care."

Anonymous

This leads to a discussion of crisis communication, arguably the most challenging area of public relations, particularly in this era of 24-hour news coverage. What was previously one-shot coverage of an event may now be shown repeatedly during the day-long news cycle.

Consider a small business that delivers fuel oil to homes. The owner finds the media outside his door after a tanker truck spills fuel in a neighborhood. Or even worse, is involved in a fatal accident. Reporters want a statement and "no comment," is almost always seen negatively by the press and the public because it implies guilt.

Imagine a worst case scenario that could affect you and your reputation. Here's another: your phone rings and a reporter asks what you can tell him about the fire one of your technicians caused in an apartment building this afternoon causing injuries to a half-dozen people and the relocation of 20 families.

This is the first you've heard of it. What you would say, knowing your response is on the record? Would you refuse to answer and refer the caller to your lawyer? Do you have a plan or would you just wing it?

After you recover from the initial shock, the key is organization. There's nothing wrong with thanking the reporter for the heads up, writing down the questions, noting his or her deadline, and promising to call back. But make certain you do call back if you promised to do so. Make certain someone makes a record of all such calls and contact information.

This honest response will provide you breathing room to gather the facts, pull your team together and decide to work with the media individually or call a press conference. This may sound simple, but if no one has preplanned this scenario chances are things will go wrong during a crisis.

There are few areas more sensitive to the flow of communication during a crisis than a school campus, particularly a college quad. They provide easy access, contain innumerable potential interviewees and, because of their population of youth with families from across the nation and the globe, command overwhelming viewer attention.

Following are three brief examples of crises on campus and the importance of a quick and accurate response. The first is from personal experience.

Early during my tenure as a college relations director, a tragic dormitory fire resulted in the death of one student and critical injuries to another. Local, regional and national media swarmed the campus for a week. The challenge was to provide information without suggesting the cause of the fire or commenting on the details of the tragedy. At that point nothing had been officially determined, but even afterward, discussing specifics before official findings of fact would have been a mistake.

The coverage was intense but fair. The initial reaction of a college attorney was to say little, if anything, to media swarming the campus. He was concerned about the possibility someone would respond to a speculative question and inadvertently assume liability for something we did or didn't do. He saw the press as an adversary looking for a gotcha question.

Fortunately, the college president understood the negative consequences of withholding information out of fear of making a mistake. He agreed to an interview I arranged with a regional TV station within hours of the early Sunday morning tragedy and, still in the faded jeans and T-shirt he'd thrown on when notified at 3:30 a.m., made a magnificent statement acknowledging the fire and eulogizing the loss of a precious student and the injuries of another. That heartfelt interview set the tone for subsequent coverage.

The point is, had we refused to comment at the beginning, our position of concern and determination to find the cause and do our best to prevent a recurrence would not have been represented -- or worse -- mischaracterized by others who might have taken the opportunity to criticize the school or administration for perceived past grievances.

In other words, we would have worked ourselves into an early hole of distrust by media first responders tasked with presenting a breaking story. It would have been easy to characterize us as being unresponsive, uninformed, or worse, uncaring or covering up.

I won't comment on the 32 shooting deaths at Virginia Tech in Blacksburg, Va., in April 2007 except to note that one of the primary issues repeatedly raised by the media and families was the slowness of information passed on campus during the two-hour killing spree. The Virginia Tech Review Panel, a state-appointed body assigned to review the incident, criticized college administrators for failing to take timely action that may have reduced the number of casualties.

A more recent campus tragedy occurred at Delaware State University at the start of the fall 2007 semester. Two students were shot at random on campus by another student. The incident occurred around one a.m., on a Friday morning as students were leaving a campus snack bar.

Adding to the confusion, the university is located on US13 across the highway from Dover International Speedway, which coincidentally was swamped with more than 100,000 fans in town for two NASCAR races that weekend. There were at least a dozen local, regional and national media reps there, broadcasting live during a 45-minute impromptu press conference complete with traffic noise in the background.

Though hammered by often redundant questions about the university's history, size, population, and the events surrounding the shootings, spokesman Carlos Holmes continually incorporated reassurances that the campus was locked down and students were safe.

He knew the most important thing to parents, relatives and friends glued to TV sets across the country was that the situation was under control and no further harm would occur on campus. He held a number of follow up press conferences and media briefings as events unfolded and the alleged shooter, a freshman, was apprehended.

In addition to doors being knocked on, phone calls and text messages, the university public affairs office issued press releases. Following is one of several releases put out across campus, including on websites. The releases provided information on the incident, that classes were canceled, that non-essential personnel had been told not to report for duty, that students were to remain in their residence halls, and where additional information could be obtained. It was clear to everyone that safety was of paramount importance. Would your organization be able to react as quickly?

Delaware State University Press Release Issues September 21, 2007

TIMELY WARNING NOTIFICATION

Sept. 21, 2007 (5:10 a.m.)

Classes Canceled due to Shooting on Campus (update)

Classes on the Dover campus of Delaware State University have been canceled for Friday, Sept. 21 in the wake of an early morning shooting at the institution that has left two students wounded and a suspect at large. All non-essential personnel are directed not to report to work on this day.

The primary priorities of the University at this point are the safety of the residential student population and the DSU Police investigation of the shooting. DSU Police Department with the assistance of the Dover Police Department are working toward the apprehension of the suspect.

The university is implementing a plan to provide essential services to its residential population on campus. Because the suspect is still at large, residential students are directed to remain in their residence halls for their safety until further notice.

At approximately 12:54 a.m. on Friday, Sept. 21, the Delaware State University Police Department was notified of an incident in which two students were shot on campus near Memorial Hall. A single male suspect is being sought, but has not yet been apprehended. The investigation is continuing with the assistance of other local police.

A male student and a female student were transported to hospitals within the state. The male student is in stable condition, however, the female student's injuries are considered serious.

University personnel and students can check of updates on this situation through the DSU Website (www.desu.edu) and through the DSU Snow Phone # at ... "

###

Regardless of the setting of a tragedy, families and friends want to know someone is in control and their loved ones are being protected. Depending on the type, size, or risks involved in your business, a basic crisis plan should be in place. It's too late when police, fire and rescue vehicles are on the scene.

Large industries have crisis plans that incorporate both physical safety and media contact procedures. They can be very complex and include employee phone trees, medical triage, backup communication channels and locations, and emergency notification procedures. For plans to work as designed, they must be practiced and updated.

If you run a business where an accident or disaster could cause widespread casualties or property damage, you absolutely should have a plan to work with the media to assist them in getting the word out to affected internal and external stakeholders. If you stumble at the beginning of the communication process your reputation may be left in tatters.

Include the following elements in your crisis planning:

- Designated and recognized spokespersons who not only coordinate and provide regular media and internal briefings as the situation unfolds, but who also brief others to speak on company issues like security, safety, and personnel matters.

- Contact information on all spokespersons, including new phone numbers specifically designated for the media.

- A policy that bad news will never be withheld but given up front and completely. To do otherwise risks your credibility and forces reporters to seek out other sources of information. However, make certain your information is correct before you release it. Don't draw broad conclusions based on a limited amount of information.

- A log of media contacts and press releases. It provides a history of what was said, who said it, and to whom it was said. It will prove valuable in post-event debriefings and follow up, including possible legal issues.

- A method to get information to a lot of people simultaneously, including mass text messaging capability, emergency phone numbers reserved for a crisis, and a preprogrammed Internet "black site" containing routine and emergency information that can be brought on line during a crisis.

- A plan for periodic training of all employees about the plan, how the company will carry it out, and what is expected of them.

All employees should be briefed on and be familiar with the plan, including relaying media queries to company spokespersons. A loose cannon who doesn't know what's going on but is willing to talk to any reporter may be portrayed as your company's spokesperson and dig you in deep. Conversely, a good plan assures employees and external audiences that management has a handle on the situation and is in charge.

Practice the plan. That includes setting up simulated interviews with hostile questions, i.e., "Why didn't you anticipate this and take preventative action?" "Don't you feel guilty so many people are suffering because of what your company did?" "Whose fault is this?" What is your responsibility in this and what do you have to say to the family who lost its father?" These questions and worse have all been asked and should be anticipated.

Never assume you can walk into a press conference and just wing it. Bring notes with oversize type with you to the podium. Make certain your notes contain the key points you want to deliver so none are missed if you get distracted. Never show anger or assume tough or repetitive questions are personal. Remember that your audience is not the seemingly overly aggressive reporter, but his or her readers and viewers. In fact, remaining cool and even-tempered will always work in your favor.

When you provide briefings about an unfolding negative event, say what needs to be said and stop. One of the methods some reporters use to encourage someone to keep talking is to hold the microphone in front of the subject's mouth after he or she has given a statement. The temptation to fill the silence is enormous. Be careful.

A rule of thumb in being interviewed about a contentious subject is not to make assumptions about what you're being asked and go off on a tangent to areas where you're no longer comfortable or qualified. Your goal is to pass information along in a dialogue with the media rather than downloading vast quantities of irrelevant information that will confuse the issue.

Venturing too deeply into crisis planning is a specialized area and not the intent of this primer. Depending on the type of business, plans can be complex and involved but need to be in place to preserve life and reputation.

Finally, think about what your response would be in an unexpected situation, including the on-the-job death of an employee or members of the public. Your response may determine whether you maintain public trust or even remain in business. Tom Peters, co-author of the classic management handbook, *In Search of Excellence*, put it this way: "There is no such thing as a minor lapse of integrity."

In Closing ...

"If a man is called to be a streetsweeper, he should sweep even as Michelangelo painted. He should sweep streets so well that all the hosts of heaven and earth will pause to say, 'Here lived a great streetsweeper.'"

Dr. Martin Luther King, Jr., Baptist minister, civil rights leader

I'll close with these simple thoughts.

- Always remember you are an expert in what you do. There has never been anyone like you and there never will be.

- You are your own best advocate. Never miss an opportunity to let people know what you do and how well you do it.

- Once you become a public figure be on your best behavior both on and off duty.

- Always speak kindly of others.

- Laugh a lot. Smile when you're stressed. Smile harder when you're angry. People will flock to you.

They'll also wonder what you're up to.

Dave Skocik

PS: For those who would like to continue the dialogue and share your own stories of insight and success please e-mail me at info@davidskocik.com. I'd love to include some of them in a book in progress on the genius class of entrepreneurs who make America work!

About the Author

Dave Skocik holds a master's degree in communication from Temple University and is nationally accredited by the Public Relations Society of America, for which he's served as a state chapter president, mid-Atlantic district chair, and as a national educational committee member. PRSA, the world's premier and largest organization of PR professionals, has 32,000 professional and student members.

His more than 25 years experience in public relations working with diverse audiences includes 11 years as an executive director of college relations and assistant professor of communication. He is president of PR Delaware LLC, a consulting business in Dover, Delaware. His business website is www. PRDelaware.com

Dave also served in the Delaware Army National Guard and later in the Navy Reserve as a public affairs specialist. In January 2005 he was chosen as the military parade announcer for the White House reviewing stand at President Bush's inauguration. He retired from military service in December 2007.

Experienced in electronic media, he has been a radio announcer and has co-produced and hosted an award-winning TV quiz show for Delaware high school students since 1987, and also serves as the official word pronouncer for the annual state spelling bee, grades 4 to 8, in addition to many community-based emcee roles.

Perhaps most relevant to his readers is that he's been a mechanical contractor who understands the challenges involved with running a small business and working with employees and the public.

He welcomes and encourages feedback on this book at info@davidskocik. com.

www.ingramcontent.com/pod-product-compliance
Lightning Source LLC
Chambersburg PA
CBHW030858180526
45163CB00004B/1623